T0149822

This book is book is available in quantity at special discounts for your group or organization.
For further information, contact:

Triumph Books LLC
814 North Franklin Street
Chicago, Illinois 60610
Phone: (312) 337-0747
www.triumphbooks.com

Star Tribune
This book was based on news stories and columns that were written on Adrian Peterson's knee injury, rehabilitation and comeback season of 2012.

Printed in U.S.A.
ISBN: 978-1-60078-900-7

Content packaged by Mojo Media, Inc.
Joe Funk: Editor
Jason Hinman: Creative Director

Cover photos by Carlos Gonzalez/Star Tribune

CARLOS GONZALEZ, Star Tribune

CONTENTS

INTRODUCTION

In 2012, Adrian Peterson altered our perspective.

By JIM SOUHAN/STAR TRIBUNE

GOOD ATHLETES change the game in which they play.

In 2012, Adrian Peterson altered the way we look at modern running backs, and athletes recovering from major knee surgery. He altered the way we look at his franchise, and his career arc.

He changed perceptions like an illusionist while working in the harsh realm of reality.

As recently as August, a rational observer could have seen in Peterson a worn-down running back eight months removed from surgery to repair his anterior cruciate and medial collateral ligaments playing for an inept NFL team against defenses that would have little trouble choking the line of scrimmage.

A rational observer could have suggested that Peterson wasn't fully prepared to play in the first game of the season.

In that first game, against Jacksonville, Peterson roared to the crowd during introductions, took the field with the starting lineup and scored two touchdowns.

He spent six games proving he was healthy, and the rest of the season proving he's one of the greatest backs of all time. During an eight-game stretch he produced these rushing totals: 153, 123, 182, 171, 108, 210, 154 and 212.

Houston held him to 86 yards in the penultimate game of the season, leaving him with 1,898 yards entering the finale against Green Bay. He rushed for 199 against the Packers, falling nine yards shy of Eric Dickerson's record, but leading the Vikings into the playoffs.

So in his first season after undergoing knee surgery, he led the NFL in rushing while threatening a record and changing the way we think about running backs, or at least one running back.

Recent NFL history has taught us that good NFL backs are interchangeable, and that their exploits are not a direct cause of team success. The NFL has become a passing league. Great quarterbacks elevate entire franchises and win titles and that great running backs shine briefly for mediocre teams before their bodies give out.

Recent sports history has taught us that while modern surgeons work miracles, top athletes normally require a year of on-the-field recovery before recapturing their form. Peterson shattered that notion by taking brutal hits, moving piles of bodies, sprinting away from safeties and cutting laterally as if commanded by a joystick.

Recent Vikings history suggested winning would require a long rebuilding process, one that would threaten to squander Peterson's prime.

Recent history has taught us that quarterbacks are far more valuable than running backs, because a defense intent on stopping one runner almost always succeeds.

A recent history of running backs suggested that prime could be shortened by sheer physics: The size and speed of the players hitting Peterson today was unimaginable during Jim Brown's prime.

Peterson has proved the exception to many supposed rules. About one year after shredding his knee in Washington, D.C., Peterson has reclaimed his place

Peterson rehabilitates his injury in May 2012. JERRY HOLT, Star Tribune

as the NFL's best running back while speeding his franchise's return to competitiveness.

He has simultaneously elevated the position he plays, and the franchise for which he plays.

With the Vikings proving frequently incapable of completing passes downfield, defenses massed at the line of scrimmage, daring Peterson to run. If ever a ``prevent run defense'' becomes fashionable in the NFL, it will be because Peterson frustrated so many teams intent on stopping him in the backfield.

One of the most insipid clichés in sports is that one athlete puts a team "literally on his back."

We can, though, reshape the metaphor to work for Peterson. Among the many exercises he performed to prepare himself for this season, he would sprint with a sled or a parachute trailing him, increasing the resistance of each step.

This season, Peterson has sprinted ahead, taking all sorts of people along for the ride.

He seems oblivious to the added weight.

Or maybe he just likes the challenge. ■

Knee Deep in Agony

Peterson suffered a torn ACL in his left knee as the Vikings beat Washington.

By DAN WIEDERER/STAR TRIBUNE • December 25, 2011

LANDOVER, MD. — In many ways, Christmas 2011 for the Vikings should have been defined by an inspiring slogan, an 11-word adage delivered by Joe Webb from the postgame podium at FedEx Field.

"Stay prepared," Webb said. "And when your opportunity comes, take advantage of it."

In a perfect world, Webb's words would have been the neat way for the Vikings to package their 33-26 victory over the Washington Redskins, as the backup quarterback sparked a second-half eruption with three touchdowns.

Yet Webb was only a small part of the story. The far more significant scene from an otherwise pleasant Christmas Eve came on the first play after halftime. That's when Adrian Peterson took a handoff from Christian Ponder and was drilled in the left knee by Redskins safety DeJon Gomes.

Peterson's left leg was planted at the time and had little give. Instead, it bent sideways and left the Vikings superstar face down on the grass writhing in agony.

A magnetic resonance imaging exam Saturday night confirmed Peterson suffered a torn anterior cruciate ligament. That injury could keep Peterson from being available to the Vikings at the start of the 2012 season.

His first thoughts?

"Oh Lord," Peterson said after the game, before he received the diagnosis. "I just knew something bad happened."

Percy Harvin knew immediately Peterson was in trouble, promptly waving for the Vikings medical staff to rush out.

"You don't ever want to see that," Harvin said. "As soon as he went down, with the pain he was grimacing with, you know something was wrong. ... I kind of [glanced at] his whole body, saw his leg and knew it was bad."

Peterson seemed downright disconsolate as he stood on crutches and talked to reporters in the locker room after the game. Both he and the team were bracing for the worst. The Vikings said coach Leslie Frazier would give a further update on the injury Monday.

"Some people told me what they saw on TV and they said it looked pretty bad," Frazier said immediately after the game. "I'm just hoping and praying it's not what I'm being told."

As if Peterson's injury wasn't bad enough, on the next play Ponder took a vicious shot to the head while being sacked by Adam Carriker and London Fletcher, producing concussion-like symptoms that ended the rookie quarterback's day.

But this is where a woeful season -- the Vikings (3-12) seemed to be in the hunt for the No. 1 overall draft choice if they lost their final two games and Indianapolis won next week -- has its silver lining, however small.

This was a lesson in patience, an uplifting moment for a 25-year-old reserve who seems to always respond when called upon.

This was a victory that ended a six-game losing streak

Vikings staff members assist Peterson off the field. CARLOS GONZALEZ, Star Tribune

and left the Vikings feeling encouraged as they headed home for the holidays, with a little satisfaction.

"This is not relief," linebacker Chad Greenway said. "This is a celebration. It's our third win and we're excited about it no matter what anyone else thinks."

The jubilation was mostly thanks to Webb, who for the second time in three weeks took over the huddle and injected it with all sorts of positive energy.

The result: four consecutive second-half scoring drives that proved this mediocre team's continued resolve.

With Ponder out, Webb strutted into the huddle and turned up the energy. He rushed for 34 yards, including a nifty 9-yard scoring run in which he delivered an Xbox cutback past Reed Doughty. Webb also completed four of his five passes for 84 yards, including a 17-yard TD toss to tight end Kyle Rudolph and an 8-yarder to Harvin.

"Magic," Harvin said. "Joe's gifted. He's one of those gifted players who does things you can't describe."

With Peterson down, Toby Gerhart responded as well, rushing for 109 yards on 11 carries. His 67-yard run, which came two plays before Webb's scoring sprint, was the Vikings' longest rush of the season.

To be clear, this was by no means a masterful performance. At times, the Washington offense seemed high-powered on the way to 397 total yards. Rookie Evan Royster rushed for 132 yards on 19 carries. Rex Grossman threw for 284 yards with two touchdown passes.

But despite a rash of shaky tackling, the defense also delivered a few big plays. Brian Robison's strip sack of Grossman in the first quarter led to a 36-yard Ryan Longwell field goal.

Mistral Raymond, meanwhile, helped thwart Washington's attempt to rally with an interception with 7:32 to play, the Vikings' first pick in 76 days.

Peterson's agony could have deflated this team, a group that has experienced a wide array of misfortune in 2011. Instead, the Vikings absorbed the adversity and dug deep.

"I think everybody just rallied," Harvin said. "I know personally, what was going through my mind, I was like, 'Just forget all this mess, man. Let's go out and get this win no matter what it takes.' I'm assuming that's what the rest of the team was thinking."

Now, the Vikings are left to spend Christmas thinking about Peterson's devastating injury and his suddenly uncertain future. ■

Adrian Peterson leaves the field with a knee injury in the third quarter. CARLOS GONZALEZ, Star Tribune

Ugly Play Leads to Even Uglier Diagnosis

Adrian Peterson tore a knee ligament: 'I just knew it was something bad.'

By JIM SOUHAN/STAR TRIBUNE • December 25, 2011

LANDOVER, MD. — In the NFL, a league filled with violence and severe injuries, it takes a lot to make people wince. When Adrian Peterson went down on Saturday, even players recoiled.

Peterson, the Vikings' star running back, took a handoff on Saturday. As he hit the hole, Redskins safety DeJon Gomes smashed into Peterson's left knee from the side. There was little doubt about the severity of the injury, and late Saturday the Vikings announced that an MRI revealed a torn anterior cruciate ligament.

Peterson, known for his toughness, writhed on the ground, his left leg limp. Redskins players removed their helmets and knelt. People in the press box recoiled while watching the replay.

"I just knew it was something bad," Peterson said later, in the locker room, while leaning on crutches.

Peterson underwent an X-ray on Saturday at FedEx Field, ruling out the possibility of broken bones, but later the MRI showed the torn ACL. It's likely to require surgery and a lengthy rehabilitation that could affect the beginning of the 2012 season. Coach Leslie Frazier will discuss the injury during a news conference Sunday.

"You take a blow to the knee like that, you're concerned about the ACL and the MCL, those ligaments, mainly," Peterson said just after the game. "I'm just trying to stay positive as I can."

Peterson said the injury was "very severe, painwise."

He said he had no regrets, playing in what was essentially a meaningless game. In September, Peterson signed a seven-year contract worth $100 million. At 26, he is a franchise player who plays a position known for wearing out most stars by the age of 30.

"Not at all," he said when asked if he questioned whether he should have played. "I felt like I was healthy enough to go and be productive."

Peterson missed three games because of a high ankle sprain before returning last week, when he carried 10 times for 60 yards against New Orleans. Saturday, he rushed 12 times for 38 yards and one touchdown before his injury.

He finishes the season with 970 rushing yards, 30 shy of reaching 1,000 yards for the fifth time in his five NFL seasons.

"I felt good coming out the second half, man," he said. "I just had more energy and I was ready to really get things going. But, unfortunately, it was cut short on the first play."

The play was remindful of a hit that Packers cornerback Al Harris made on Peterson during his rookie season. In that case, Harris appeared to target Peterson's knee. "I do remember that one," Peterson said. "Thank God my knee wasn't planted. Unfortunately, my knee was planted on this one."

Backup running back Toby Gerhart rushed 11 times for 109 yards, including a 67-yard run. ▪

CARLOS GONZALEZ, Star Tribune

Vikings trainer Eric Sugarman
along with coach Leslie Frazier
and team personnel tend to
Peterson after his injury.
MCKENNA EWEN, Star Tribune

Peterson, on Crutches, Facing Long Road to Recovery

The premier tailback is trying to be upbeat after a horrific knee injury.

By DAN WIEDERER/STAR TRIBUNE • December 26, 2011

HE SEEMED LOST, in a daze like never before. Balancing on crutches in the visitor's locker room of FedEx Field on Saturday evening, Adrian Peterson didn't really know what to say.

He had yet to undergo the MRI that would later reveal major ligament damage in his left knee, an ACL tear with MCL problems also likely.

But it was clear from Peterson's blank expression that he had seen his future flash before his eyes.

He seemed depressed. Confused. A little scared even.

Before even saying a word, Peterson stared into the carpet and let his lips rumble with exasperation.

No one in the Vikings' locker room would say it. But the vibe was apparent, that one monstrous unanswerable question hovering in the air like stale cigar smoke: Had we seen the last of Adrian Peterson?

Not in the sense that Peterson never will play again. No one in the Vikings organization has the stomach to even consider that fate at this early stage of the injury. But if and when Peterson can return to action, will this injury sap him of his trademark explosiveness?

Did this one fluke play in a meaningless game late in a terrible season signal a premature decline for one of the most electric playmakers in team history?

It's far too early to foster much of an educated guess.

But the fact these questions are being asked should give one a sense of the situation's gravity and a better understanding of the suffering Peterson seemed to be experiencing Christmas Eve.

After all, if you thought the hit he took from DeJon Gomes looked bad, with Peterson's knee buckling and turning in all the wrong directions, you should have felt the pain that came with it.

"Was it as bad as it looked? Yeah," Peterson said. "Especially initially, the pain was very severe."

Now comes the mental agony, too, that paralyzing uncertainty of what's next, the curiosity surrounding the recovery timetable.

The range of possibilities is wide. Yes, the most optimistic Vikings fans will gravitate toward the belief that this is merely a minor setback for a star as tough as Peterson.

They'll immediately reference Wes Welker. After all, the Patriots receiver tore both his ACL and MCL on Jan. 3, 2010. Yet, miraculously he was back playing full-time by the middle of the preseason 8 1/2 months later.

Less than two years removed from that injury, Welker appears to be better than ever, leading the NFL with 116 receptions and having set a Patriots single-season record for receiving yards (1,518 and counting).

That has to provide a nice ray of hope for Peterson, right?

"I'm going to try to stay as positive as I possibly can," he promised Saturday.

Still, the pessimist line is swelling with concrete examples that validate the worst fears.

Remember the catastrophic knee injury quarterback Daunte Culpepper suffered at Carolina early in the 2005 season?

At the time, he was a 28-year-old budding superstar coming off a Pro Bowl season during which he set a new NFL record for yards from scrimmage.

Then, after one fluke play, he plummeted from game-changing to ordinary.

Yes, Culpepper stuck around the NFL for the next four seasons. But he was never the same, physically weakened and just a little uncertain of his knee's strength.

After that injury, Culpepper started only 20 games for three different teams over four seasons and was last seen playing for the Sacramento Mountain Lions of the United Football League.

So yeah, the naysayers see Welker's impressive recovery pushed to the center of the conversation but quickly raise you a Culpepper, a Keith Millard, a Terrell Davis, a Jamal Anderson, a Cadillac Williams and a Robert Edwards, all players whose blown knees stole their dynamic abilities right in their prime.

Davis, like Peterson, was in his fifth NFL season at the time he blew his knee out in 1999.

A former MVP and two-time Super Bowl champ, he was never a difference-maker again, plagued by knee problems plus additional injuries and playing only 13 more games in 2000 and 2001 before calling it quits.

No wonder Peterson seemed so crestfallen Saturday, struggling to come to grips with what had just happened. He knew the injury was bad. Perhaps, even worse, he understood it will take an incredibly long time to determine just how bad.

What a year.

On Sept. 10, on the Vikings' first road trip this season, Peterson was given a seven-year contract extension worth $100 million. The future seemed bright.

Fifteen weeks later, on the final trip of 2011, he absorbed a career-threatening knee injury, suddenly lined up for surgery, a grueling rehabilitation process and an immediate future with so much doubt attached. ■

Peterson leaves FedEx Field on a cart after his knee injury. MCKENNA EWEN, Star Tribune

Vikings' Goal: Peterson Playing in 2012 Opener

The team hopes its star will miss only one game after knee injury.

By MARK CRAIG/STAR TRIBUNE • December 27, 2011

IT WAS A CHRISTMAS DAY conversation between a coach and a devastated player, a coach whose playing career was cut short 25 years ago by the same injury the player now carries with him into an uncertain future.

The two had spoken the night before, on a plane bound for Minneapolis-St. Paul from Washington, D.C. But the coach, Leslie Frazier, felt the need to double back less than a day later with another uplifting message because he remembers the extent to which an NFL player's "mental fortitude" is tested in the first 24 hours following a torn anterior cruciate ligament.

The Vikings coach shared that message publicly on Monday as he and Eric Sugarman, the team's head athletic trainer, went before the media to paint a promising picture that, they believe, realistically includes running back Adrian Peterson returning to his four-time All-Pro form in time for the start of the 2012 regular season.

"Adrian and I talked," Frazier said, "and I told him that he'll be the guy that people will look at and say, 'Wow, look at Adrian Peterson. He's just as good or better than he was before the surgery.'"

According to Sugarman, Peterson also tore the medial collateral ligament, which is common when the ACL is torn. There also was damage to the medial and lateral meniscus but no damage to the posterior cruciate and lateral collateral ligaments, or to the chondral surface, or cartilage, which Sugarman said was a "positive thing for this injury."

Peterson will have surgery in a week to 10 days, once the swelling subsides and his range of motion is restored. The team's hopes are for Peterson to rehab in Minnesota during the offseason. Peterson wasn't available for comment Monday.

Sugarman said most players today are expected to recover from this injury in eight to nine months. The regular season will start about eight months after Peterson has his surgery.

Sugarman also warned people not to compare Peterson to other players who have had this injury.

"I would really like Adrian to stand on his own merit because Adrian, I feel, is very unique," Sugarman said. "If there's anyone that's going to be able to recover from this injury, it's Adrian Peterson. ... Adrian has a great work ethic. Adrian has the DNA to heal quickly, which he has shown in the past. And he certainly will have the desire and the mental toughness to be able to get through the rehab process."

The team's goal is to have Peterson ready for the regular-season opener. If that comes to fruition, the gruesome blow delivered by Redskins safety DeJon Gomes in Saturday's 33-26 victory will have cost Peterson only one game, Sunday's season finale vs. the Bears.

Frazier said the team's offense, which is being built around Peterson, won't have to be changed. He said the team is counting on Peterson's return, adding that back-

up Toby Gerhart, who had his first 100-yard game (109) on Saturday, has proven he can fill in if Peterson needs a little more time to come back.

Peterson, who went into the regular season with the smile of a man who had just signed a seven-year, $100 million extension, looked understandably sad when seen outside the team's practice facility Monday. Frazier, however, said he sensed by the end of their Christmas Day conversation that Peterson had "begun to move forward" and was "not down in the dumps or feeling sorry for himself."

And unlike Frazier, whose career as a cornerback ended a quarter-century ago in the Bears' Super Bowl XX victory, Peterson's injury has occurred at a time when the marvels of modern medicine have made comebacks commonplace.

"One of the things that Adrian had mentioned to Eric and others, to the fans, was to stay positive because he is going to remain positive," Frazier said. "He is extremely positive about being able to come back and be as good or better than he was before, and that's the Adrian we're all accustomed to seeing. He sets his goals extremely high and he's one of those guys who, when he puts his mind to it, there's no reason to ever doubt that he can't achieve what he really puts his mind to." ■

Peterson sits on the bench after his injury against the Redskins. CARLOS GONZALEZ, Star Tribune

Peterson to Undergo Knee Surgery Today

By MARK CRAIG/STAR TRIBUNE • December 30, 2011

ADD VIKINGS running back Adrian Peterson to the list of elite athletes who have asked Dr. James Andrews to put them back together.

Andrews, considered the foremost orthopedic surgeon when it comes to rebuilding elbows, shoulders and knees, will operate on Peterson's left knee Friday at the Andrews Sports Medicine Orthopedics Center at St. Vincent's Medical Center in Birmingham, Ala.

Peterson, who tore the anterior cruciate and medial collateral ligaments in Saturday's victory at Washington, will return to Minnesota on Monday. Coach Leslie Frazier said he and Peterson will discuss how much of the rehabilitation is done in Minnesota and how much is done at Peterson's home near Houston.

Frazier clearly has a preference.

"You like for guys to be at your facility, with your doctors and your trainers and people here," Frazier said. "But at the same time, if a guy is set up in a situation where we'd feel like the people who are working with him are qualified and doing the same type of protocol that we would have, then you'll work with them on getting that done. But ideally, you'd like them to be at your facility."

The Who's Who list of athletes who have been going to Andrews the past three-plus decades is lengthy. Troy Aikman, Charles Barkley, Michael Jordan, Jack Nicklaus, Emmitt Smith, to name a few. And Drew Brees, whose career was in jeopardy back in 2005.

As for Peterson, Frazier said the two talked Thursday, "and he's in good spirits. He's anxious to get the surgery done and get started on his rehab." ■

RENEE JONES SCHNEIDER, Star Tribune

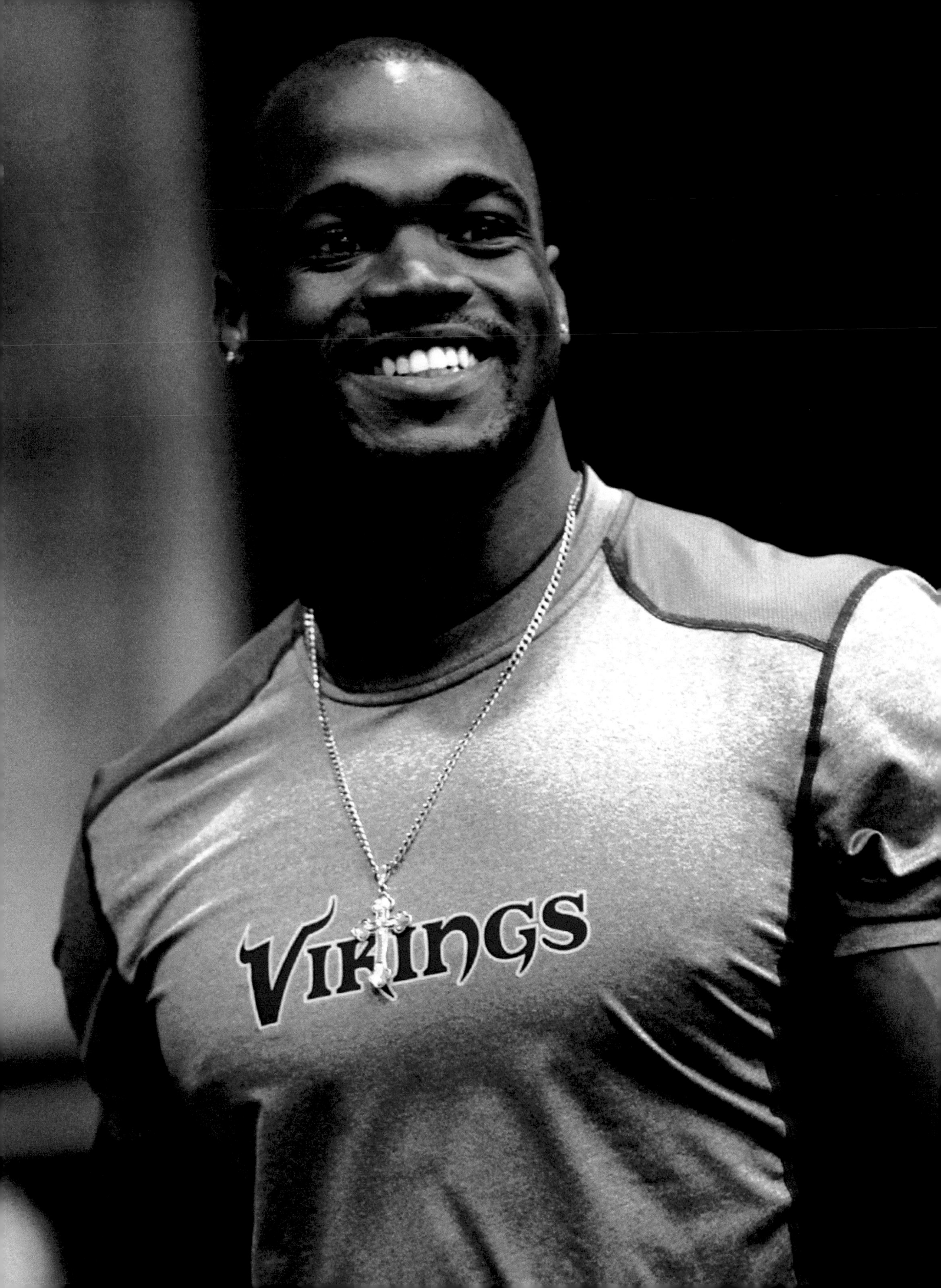
VIKINGS

Six days after his injury, Peterson had surgery. CARLOS GONZALEZ, Star Tribune

Peterson Still Making Moves

Impressive progress made in his rehabilitation but needs patience in the next phases.

By DAN WIEDERER/STAR TRIBUNE • January 14, 2012

YES, ADRIAN PETERSON has watched the replay footage of that fateful and seemingly routine third-quarter run from Christmas Eve in Maryland. Just thinking about it causes the Vikings running back to recoil and cringe as if he has just downed a glass of curdled milk.

Everyone knows how that sequence turned out, Peterson planting at the wrong instant with Redskins safety DeJon Gomes arriving at the same moment and delivering a hit that turned Peterson's left leg into a pipe cleaner.

Just like that, Peterson tore his anterior cruciate and medial collateral ligaments.

"My stomach crawls just looking at it," Peterson said. "Your leg is not supposed to go that way. At all."

Yet aside from that unpleasant revisiting of a career-altering moment, Peterson proved cheerful and optimistic when he met with reporters Friday at Winter Park to discuss his rehabilitation.

Just two weeks removed from surgery, Peterson has now completed the first phase of what Vikings head athletic trainer Eric Sugarman calls a five-phase recovery process.

Peterson has begun restrengthening his quadriceps while also working on his range of motion. And he impressed Sugarman this week with his efforts on a stationary bike, showing great extension and flexion.

The agonizing postoperative pain that caused Peterson more than a few sleepless nights has subsided. Gone, too, is the self-pity and hypothetical reflection that had consumed him immediately following the injury.

"Oh, trust me, I went through that," Peterson said. "[I was like], 'Dang, what if I would have kept [the run] front side? Or 'If I would have done some ropes during the week, maybe I would have been able to get my foot up faster when I made that cut.' But it happened, man. I just figured what are the odds?"

But now the focus has turned to the road ahead and a recovery process Sugarman is overseeing with great care. Sugarman readily acknowledges his biggest chore between now and the fall will be retaining Peterson's patience.

Yes, the star running back is promising to attack his rehabilitation with great vigor. But Sugarman also knows he'll inevitably have to pull the reins back.

"We're not in a race," Sugarman said. "We're not go-

BRIAN PETERSON, Star Tribune

22

ing to rush him. We're not trying to jump to all the different phases. We're following the protocol that's prescribed for him and everyone that's had an ACL tear."

For what it's worth, Peterson is now walking without crutches and also had his surgery sutures removed. These are what Sugarman would classify as two "little victories" in a recovery process that will be full of them.

Phase 2 of the rehab will take place over the next two weeks with Peterson continuing to test his range of motion and working toward shedding the bulky brace he's wearing.

From there, the ensuing six to eight weeks will be geared toward working through a critical stage in which Peterson's replacement ligament will naturally be at its weakest.

"That's the one thing where you really have to be cautious in the first couple months," Sugarman said. "You can't push him too hard, otherwise you can put him at risk. He knows that. We all know that."

To be clear, at present Peterson's rehab remains in the very early stages. But Sugarman also asserted again that he hopes to have Peterson ready to play by Week 1 of next season, a lofty goal the running back has set and intends to reach.

Said Sugarman: "If we can meet it, that's great. We're going to strive for it until someone tells us we can't."

By May, Peterson should be on track to enter the fifth and longest phase of the recovery process. That's a stage, Sugarman said, "when you don't have really many restrictions at all as far as what you can and can't do safely. But then, of course, it just takes several months to get all your strength back, get your function back, get your agility back and all that power and burst."

Peterson has no problems admitting he questioned his ill fate immediately after he tore his ACL. But now he's reached a point of acceptance.

"It was meant to happen," he said, "because it happened."

Yet with that acceptance, Peterson also stressed he will not be slowed by skeptics who wonder if he will ever be the same explosive player he was for his first five NFL seasons.

"I feel like I'm going to come back better than before," Peterson said. "I know people might laugh at that or think otherwise. But you know what? It doesn't matter what they think or how they feel about it. The only thing that matters is how I feel about it and what I believe." ■

JERRY HOLT, Star Tribune

Frazier to Peterson: Don't Force It

By DAN WIEDERER/STAR TRIBUNE • February 25, 2012

INDIANAPOLIS — Vikings head coach Leslie Frazier spoke with Adrian Peterson on Thursday, just another regular check-in with his star running back. Only Peterson, fully aware Frazier was hard at work at the NFL combine, wasn't shy about offering advice.

"He had his GM hat on," Frazier said. "He was telling me who we should be thinking about drafting. He tends to do that. He'll call me up and text me, 'Hey, have you seen this guy? You need to.' I'm like, 'Man. What's he doing?' He's a draft guru."

Or maybe it's just the requisite give-and-take. After all, Frazier had return advice for Peterson as he continues rehabilitation on his left knee: Slow down.

Friday marked two months since Peterson tore his anterior cruciate and medial collateral ligaments in a Week 16 victory at Washington. And while the early stages of recovery have gone well, Peterson's recent contention that he hoped to be running again by the end of this month made his coach recoil.

Not so fast, Frazier warned.

Peterson must first start by doing running exercises in the pool. And, according to Frazier, it may not be until the fourth or fifth month of rehab (April or May) that true hard-surface running resumes.

"He's begun to understand that he's got to listen to the doctors, with the pace that they expect him to and not try to force this because he could do more damage than he realizes," Frazier said.

Peterson's drive and optimism are admirable and all, but ... said Frazier: "Early on, he wasn't quite getting it. This was a serious injury. You have to go at the pace they're telling you to go if you want to break all these records." ■

MCKENNA EWEN, Star Tribune

Peterson Rehab Has Vikings Optimistic

The star back soon will begin running on his surgically repaired knee.

By DAN WIEDERER/STAR TRIBUNE • March 29, 2012

WEST PALM BEACH, FLA. — Vikings coach Leslie Frazier delivered the update Wednesday with obvious enthusiasm. Adrian Peterson has hit the ground running.

Peterson has returned to the Twin Cities this week to begin the next phase of his knee rehabilitation. A little more than 12 weeks since having surgery to repair torn anterior cruciate and medial collateral ligaments in his left knee, the star running back has been cleared to try running on land again.

Peterson is doing so this week under the watchful eye of head athletic trainer Eric Sugarman at Winter Park.

Frazier's assessment nearly three months into Peterson's rehab? Yes, it's still early. But so far, so good.

"Everything he's done up to this point has been very good," Frazier said. "So we're hoping once he starts running he'll stay on course as well."

At this point, that eye-opening and ambitious timeline Peterson set for his return has not had to be altered. The Vikings likely will open their 2012 season Sept. 9. And everyone within the organization still hopes Peterson will be able to play that day.

"That's what we're aiming for," Frazier said. "That's what he wants to see happen. That's what we'd all love to see happen. At the same time, we'll have to be smart and see where he is. This is the beginning stages of his running. So we'll have a better gauge in another one or two weeks as to what kind of progress he's going to make.

"We need to determine, is he going to have any swelling after the first time he runs and then when he begins cutting and turning and twisting? It's a long road ahead."

SINKING IN, BOUNCING BACK

FOR FRAZIER, the severity of Peterson's injury didn't immediately register when Peterson took a handoff on the first play after halftime on Christmas Eve and felt his knee pop after a hit by Redskins cornerback DeJon Gomes.

Peterson's agony seemed obvious as he laid face down and twitching, his injured left leg bent like a pipe cleaner. Yet Frazier had a game to coach. So he wasn't able to fully wrap his brain around what had happened to his franchise running back until he had a chance to visit with Peterson on the flight home.

"To see the emotions in his face, that's when it began to sink in a little bit for me, that this was a career-threatening injury," Frazier said. "He's such a special guy. And I have such a personal affinity for him, it just made me determined, being around him at that moment, that if anyone can make it back, this guy can. But at the same time, you felt a sense of loss to a degree."

Peterson's expression on that sobering flight remains ingrained in Frazier's mind.

"He was pretty strong and trying to be encouraging," Frazier said. "But you could tell something was missing.

He's such a jubilant guy, especially after a win. And he was so serious as we were having this conversation."

ON THE RISE

IT WASN'T LONG before Peterson transformed the acceptance of his injury into a fiery ambition to return to full strength as quickly as possible. Yet Frazier, Sugarman and the therapists Peterson has been working with in Houston have issued consistent reminders that the driven running back can't rush the recovery timeline.

Slowly but surely, that message has sunk in, enabling Peterson's progress to remain on an upward climb. To this point, Frazier said, Peterson has "exceeded expectations." But the operative phrase there is "to this point."

"It's too early right now to say that he's going to abso-

lutely make it back by the first game," Frazier said. "But so far, he's on target with everything we've asked him to do."

In the meantime, Frazier and General Manager Rick Spielman continue hunting for added backfield depth. The Vikings are firm in their belief that Toby Gerhart can be a reliable starter in Peterson's absence. But having let Lorenzo Booker go in free agency, the search for a third back will continue.

So, too, will the team's ongoing evaluations of Peterson's recuperation.

Said Frazier: "He's a guy who wants to defy the odds with this injury. He wants to do things when he comes back that no one with an ACL tear has ever done."

To this point, Peterson's focus and work ethic have continued to fill the Vikings' optimism tank. ■

CARLOS GONZALEZ, Star Tribune

Caution Tempers Optimism on Peterson's Return Date

The RB has a Sept. 9 target — if the head trainer approves.

By DAN WIEDERER/STAR TRIBUNE • May 9, 2012

ADRIAN PETERSON still has that optimistic goal, one he hasn't backed down from since having surgery Dec. 30 in Alabama to repair torn anterior cruciate and medial collateral ligaments in his left knee. Peterson wants to be back in action by Sept. 9, the day the Vikings open the 2012 season against Jacksonville.

Eric Sugarman has the same goal for the star running back. Only Sugarman, the Vikings' head athletic trainer, wants to attach an asterisk to all the talk of a triumphant opening day return.

"I love Adrian," Sugarman said Tuesday. "But let's make this clear: I'm still not going to be quoted as saying he's going to play in the first game. That's not fair. I don't know that."

So what about Peterson's eagerness to vocalize Sept. 9 as a potential milestone date?

"He'll keep throwing that out there. And good for him," Sugarman said. "That's great. That's obviously our goal, to get him playing the first game. But only if he's functionally safe to do it. This is our franchise. We can't be foolish about this."

On Wednesday, Peterson and Sugarman will hold a news conference to update the progress of the eager running back's rehabilitation. To save you the suspense, Sugarman's message will be straightforward: There's plenty to be encouraged by in Peterson's rehab. But there's still a long way to go before the Vikings' medical team will be ready to activate the green light.

To this point, now nearly 19 weeks removed from surgery, Peterson has attacked his recuperation without setback. He began running on land again in late March and has progressed to where he is trying to cut.

On Wednesday, he may even give the local media a glimpse into his progress by performing several rehab drills in the Winter Park field house.

Sugarman said Peterson's left quadriceps is back to about 80 percent strength. Peterson also has no swelling in his left leg and has regained normal motion.

"Now it's all the functional stuff," Sugarman said. "Which is really the hard stuff. That takes months."

Peterson's biggest steps ahead will revolve around regaining strength and learning to fully trust his knee again. He'll also keep working on making those nifty, elusive cuts that make him so dangerous.

"Right now, when he tries to stop on a dime, he looks like he's on ice," Sugarman said. "That's normal. Deceleration is the hardest thing for those guys. Now we're starting to pound all that over the next couple months -- function and deceleration. That should just take us right to where hopefully he needs to be."

Where he needs to be is back in the Vikings' starting lineup. When that will be? The trainer and the star running back may not quite see eye-to-eye on setting a date. ■

JERRY HOLT, Star Tribune

Peterson's knee in early 2012.
BRIAN PETERSON, Star Tribune

Braced for More

Peterson is at that dangerous part of rehab — feeling good enough to push it too hard.

By MARK CRAIG/STAR TRIBUNE • May 10, 2012

VIKINGS RUNNING BACK Adrian Peterson planted his left foot, made cuts as well as a superhero can in his 19th week since major knee surgery and wrapped things up by telling a few dozen reporters that he's on a hellbent beeline toward the Jacksonville Jaguars.

Doubters beware. Jaw firmly set, the four-time All-Pro said he not only plans on playing in that Sept. 9 season opener, he also expects to "be out there full throttle."

"I'm set on what my mindset is," Peterson said Wednesday after a 15-minute workout witnessed by reporters at Winter Park. "People can say what they want to say, I've got my goals. My whole life I've been setting my goals and pushing forward. I've been successful with doing that."

Peterson said he also has been smart and followed doctors' orders not to overdo it since his surgery Dec. 30. Vikings head athletic trainer Eric Sugarman agreed with that assessment.

"He realizes now that there's too much to lose by doing something foolish the past four months and the next four months," Sugarman said. "He's been pretty good. Now you have to pull back on the reins every once in a while and just remind him. But he's been pretty good about it and I'm on the record as saying that he'll continue."

According to Sugarman, surviving the third month after surgery without a setback was critical for Peterson. That's when athletes coming off ACL surgery are most likely to push too hard and tear the new ligament before it's had enough time to strengthen on its own.

Peterson admits the knee felt stronger than it probably was during that third month. But he listened to his medical staff and took the advice of teammate Chad Greenway, who had ACL surgery as a rookie in 2006.

"Chad was telling me, 'Hey, when that third month comes and you start feeling good, you are going to feel you can do more than you need to be doing,'" Peterson said.

"He cautioned me to be careful during that time to really let it rest and don't rush. He knows how I am, too. And just his mindset, he was the same way. That advice helped."

Peterson was cleared to begin cutting this week. That's why the Vikings had Peterson demonstrate some of the drills he's working on during Wednesday's workout, which was covered by NFL Network analyst and Pro Football Hall of Famer Michael Irvin.

Peterson started with a lateral drill in which he had to field a soccer ball being rolled to either side by Sugarman. He also ran circles around a large hoop,

Peterson jumps for the media on May 9. RENÉE JONES SCHNEIDER, Star Tribune

sprinted the width of the team's indoor field four times and finished with eight standing jumps to a box that was about three or four feet high. Peterson wore a knee brace for all but the sprints.

Afterward, a winded Peterson guessed he's "over 50 percent, as far as [his usual] cutting and being explosive." He looked in great shape, as usual, but said his conditioning level won't return to regular-season form until the strength and flexibility return to the knee.

As for when he'll be able to return to football activities, Sugarman said there's no set timetable because each player he's ever dealt with has been different.

"You basically just judge it on the guy's function," Sugarman said. "You know he's to the point now where he's really safe to do just about anything. We gradually ramp him up to functional activity and when we get to the point where he's comfortable and has normal strength back to the other side, or better than the other side, and can function as he needs to, then we make that decision."

Sugarman won't predict when Peterson will return, adding that it will be a team decision from General Manager Rick Spielman on down. Of course, the team already knows where Peterson stands on the issue.

"That's just the way I'm wired," Peterson said. "I've been this way since I was young, since I started playing this game at age 7. I always wanted to be the best in whatever I did — whatever sprints, lifting, whatever. Sixteen years, 17 years of that, it becomes part of you. It's just instilled in me. It's just the way I am." ▪

Adrian Peterson practiced with his trainer in front of the media after months of recovery from a torn ACL.
RENEE JONES SCHNEIDER, Star Tribune

Fast Tracking

Peterson isn't budging from his goal to play in Week 1, but team has its own schedule.

By DAN WIEDERER/STAR TRIBUNE • June 3, 2012

ERIC SUGARMAN should probably know better. But hey, sometimes you just can't help yourself.

So even though the Vikings head athletic trainer spent the past five months preaching the need to keep Adrian Peterson's superhuman ambition from becoming dangerous, occasionally he likes to press a button or two.

You know, just to check if Peterson's relentless positivity can be tested.

That's why, in the corner of the Vikings training room, a few paces from the in-pool treadmill Peterson used during the early stages of his knee rehabilitation, Sugarman took the liberty of doctoring the art.

A framed painting hangs there. In unaltered form, it portrays Peterson looking up, his gaze calm and assured.

The new version? Sugarman changed the expression, cutting the running back's head from a photo taken last Christmas Eve and taping it to the canvas. That picture, snapped moments after Peterson blew out his anterior cruciate and medial collateral ligaments at Washington, captures the Vikings star with an agonizing grimace.

Said Sugarman: "I've told Adrian once he's fully healthy again, I'll take that down."

Peterson's take?

"Everybody's got jokes. Ha ha. It's funny. But I'm se-riously getting ready to rip that picture off. When I see it, it's always a big reminder of that day. And I'm kind of tired of looking at it. I need to find me a razor blade and go to work."

Maybe this is part of the reason Peterson has attached himself so firmly to his own projected full-recovery date.

The faster Peterson heals, the sooner he can bury that painful memory from last winter.

SO PUT an "X" through Dec. 24, 2011.

Peterson is locked in on another date: Sept. 9, 2012.

That's the day the Vikings open the regular season against Jacksonville. That's now 14 weeks away.

"What I envision is to be suited up and ready to roll. Full strength," Peterson said. "Anything else? I would be cheating myself."

Still, before fast-forwarding, perhaps it's appropriate to rewind first to the New Year's Eve Peterson never wanted to experience. That night is commemorated through pictures he tweeted from a hospital bed in Birmingham, Ala., just a day after Dr. James Andrews sliced into his left knee to repair his severely damaged ACL and MCL.

In those photos, Peterson wears a playful smirk and a plastic "HAPPY NEW YEAR" derby. He has a noisemak-

er hanging from his lips and a pint of Blue Bell vanilla ice cream in his hand.

Hey, if he was going to be confined to a hospital bed as 2011 turned into 2012, why not at least deliver a good-humored spin move?

"I was feeling a little loopy," Peterson confessed. "I wanted to have a good time too and show everyone I was in good spirits and planning to handle this the best way possible. I wasn't going to sit around and sulk."

As daunting as the rehab process seemed, Peterson immediately vowed to use positive energy as his secret weapon.

"Attitude is critical with this," said Russ Paine, the physical therapist Peterson is working closely with in Houston. "If you're not really stable with who you are,

an injury like this can be a huge blow to your ego. You're the king of the hill, then all of a sudden — uh-oh.

"But Adrian? He's been energetic since the day I met him."

That's not to say there wasn't any depression. Sugarman notes that during the two weeks after surgery, Peterson's pain was intense. Moving around in slow-motion, Peterson said, proved frustrating.

The sleep deprivation made him angry.

"You think he's Adrian Peterson. Invincible. Doesn't bleed when you cut him," Sugarman said. "But for those two weeks? He was a disaster. Every morning, coming in and laying on that [trainer's] table and he was about as miserable as a human being could be. He was calling me

Peterson runs up a hill with teammate Percy Harvin during organized team activities in May.
JERRY HOLT, Star Tribune

late at night, texting me with hate messages.

"He didn't shave. He lost weight. He hurt. And I took the brunt of it."

For two weeks and two weeks only. After that, self-pity might as well have been a slow-footed, 160-pound defensive back trying to corral Peterson in the open field.

IN HOUSTON, Peterson's drive has been on full display.

Paine, one of Andrews' endorsed therapists, has a handful of NFL players he's helping rehab injuries this offseason. That group includes Packers cornerback Tramon Williams, Buccaneers defensive tackle Amobi Okoye and free-agent safety James Ihedigbo.

"Even they recognize Adrian's different," Paine said. "He has a different protoplasm than the rest of the world."

Peterson will tell anyone who listens that immediately after his surgery, doctors told him it would take three days to regain enough strength to lift his leg. Yet as that warning was being issued, Peterson was already elevating his leg.

Last month, while guiding Peterson through a balance session at Winter Park, Sugarman called for a water break. Ten minutes later, he couldn't find Peterson. Turns out the running back had bolted to pump out a few reps on the leg press.

That's been the biggest challenge for those overseeing Peterson's recovery: making sure his drive doesn't become self-destructive.

Paine faced a similar challenge in 2000 when, as an assistant team physician to the Houston Rockets, he was helping Charles Barkley work back from a torn quadriceps tendon. Barkley was always trying to accelerate the customary patient timeline.

"I'd tell him, 'Charles, you've got to do these things by the standard. I know you think you're special. But your quad tendon doesn't know it's in Charles Barkley's body,' " Paine said. "And he looked at me with a smile and said, 'Oh, yes it does.'"

Peterson is similarly wired. Darn proud of it, too.

"With the experts, I'm sure 90 or 95 percent of the time, they're right with their estimates," he said. "But there are some guys you can't put the traditional timetable on. Some guys are different. I just happen to feel I'm one of those guys."

AT THIS STAGE, Peterson has done two Winter Park rehab workouts in front of the media. The most recent came Wednesday.

Adrian Peterson pushed himself hard—no surprise there—during a parachute drill during Vikings organized team activities at Winter Park. JERRY HOLT, Star Tribune

He shuffled while chasing a soccer ball in a sand pit.

He ran sprints with receiver Percy Harvin, sprinting up a steep hill beside the practice field each time.

Peterson also ran full speed in the end zone as Sugarman restricted his progress with a parachute apparatus, then suddenly released him to run free.

"I was having a heck of a time holding him back," Sugarman said.

That's been the challenge all along.

Plus, it's only going to get harder as Peterson continues to see Vikings teammates practicing and working toward that season opener.

For now, he remains ahead of schedule. His full range of motion has returned. He looks great and feels better.

But Paine issues a reminder of the phases Peterson has yet to clear. His left quadriceps still needs strengthening. Then there's the inescapable need to regain proprioception — getting his knee to reach a state of equilibrium and balance with the rest of his body. That takes time.

So while Sugarman supports Peterson's urge to be ready for Week 1, he isn't crazy enough to promise it.

"In reality, he is only going to be back on the field when he is functionally safe to go on the field. Not just because he wants to say, 'Oh, I did it. I'm the greatest.' There's a lot more to it."

Which leads to the one question that seems to confound Peterson: What happens if Sept. 9 arrives and he is not ready to play?

"I don't know how to answer that question," Peterson said. "And I struggle to even entertain it. Because that's not the way my mind is tuned in. I can't let that negativity seep in. My mindset is that I will be there. I want to be playing. Forget what everyone else says."

OK.

So Sept. 9 remains the goal until it's no longer possible. Then, if need be, Peterson will readjust.

"No," Peterson asserted. "The goal is the goal. And I'm going to accomplish it." ◼

BRIAN PETERSON , Star Tribune

Peterson Busting to Go as Training Camp Opens

Star back will open on PUP list.

By DAN WIEDERER/STAR TRIBUNE • July 27, 2012

MANKATO, MINN. — Christian Ponder sure seems dedicated to proving he will do just about anything to help the team. On Thursday, the day the Vikings reported to training camp at Minnesota State Mankato, the second-year quarterback hung back in the Twin Cities until the early afternoon, waiting for a key passenger in his carpool.

That buddy — rookie left tackle Matt Kalil — first needed clearance before heading for Mankato.

But as the finishing details were being typed into Kalil's first contract — a four-year deal likely worth around $20 million — Ponder sprung into action, picking Kalil up at the airport, driving him directly to Winter Park to sign the paperwork, and then pointing their joyride south on Hwy. 169.

"Yeah, I call Christian up any time and he picks me up and takes me places," Kalil joked as he checked into Gage Hall.

Not that Ponder wasn't lobbying for more than just some added pocket protection. He also wanted it noted that Kalil's agent, Tom Condon, wasn't the only one instrumental in finishing the deal.

"If Tom Condon takes 3 percent of his contract, I should take at least a half a percent," Ponder said.

Anyway you spin it, Vikings fans can breathe a sigh of relief.

The team's new standout left tackle is in camp. On time. Without missing so much as a meeting, something coach Leslie Frazier asserted was "a big deal."

And that wasn't the only development Thursday that had exuberance levels high.

Another bullet dodged: Five weeks after requesting a trade and hinting his punctual arrival at training camp wasn't a given, receiver Percy Harvin checked in with no drama.

Adrian Peterson also arrived, exuding his usual gusto and vowing to return to practice as soon as the medical staff will clear him.

"I'm going to lobby to get out there and be involved some," Peterson said. "To what extent I don't know. But I feel like I can participate a little bit."

GETTING WELL FAST

PETERSON LIKELY will start camp on the physically-unable-to-perform list, a designation that can be removed at any time before the regular season starts. That means his early activity would come on the side, supervised by head athletic trainer Eric Sugarman.

Peterson, who had surgery after a serious left knee injury suffered on Christmas Eve, understood that was the most likely scenario but was still vowing to fight deep into Thursday night for his right to practice soon if not immediately.

"To be honest with you, I'm going to try to fight against [the PUP list] so I can get out there and be involved," he said. "But I know these guys are going to do what's best for this team."

In the big picture, even as the Vikings wisely use caution with Peterson, it's remarkable how far he has come

JERRY HOLT, Star Tribune

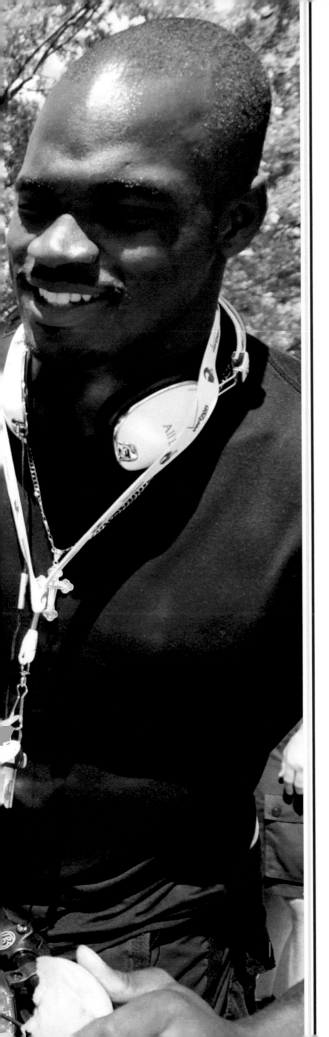

in his recovery. Monday will mark seven months since the surgery. And yet the star running back diagnosed himself Thursday as "full-go."

"I'm pretty much doing everything," he said. "Cutting. Running. Jumping. It's different when you put pads on and you have guys diving at your legs and you're making these second cuts based off the instincts of the game. So that aspect I haven't really had a lot to practice with. And that's really what I want."

Peterson's spirits won't likely be questioned at any time during camp, his needle permanently stuck on "Cheery and Optimistic." The same can't be said definitively for Harvin, who likely will undergo a requisite mood check with reporters Friday.

Upon checking into camp Thursday, Harvin didn't stop to talk. Which left Frazier to again publicly address the melodrama from June.

Frazier indicated he talked to Harvin several times in the past month, even bumping into him by surprise this week at Dick's Sports Barbers in Eden Prairie and leaving with the feeling that "all is good."

"[Our chairs] weren't right next to each other," Frazier said. "But we pulled them closer so we could be close to each other."

KEY DEVELOPMENT

FRAZIER SAID he has made it clear he wants Harvin to remain a team leader and "be the Percy that we all know." Which means that distractions like last month's mini-controversy won't easily be tolerated.

Said Frazier: "If he can continue to be that person that his teammates can trust and can count on and do the things he has done for us in the past, I won't see any problems with Percy. Because we know that he loves the game. He has a passion for the game. He wants to bring a championship to Minnesota. And when that's the case, we can all work towards the same common goal."

Right now, one of the biggest goals the Vikings have is to establish chemistry within a young team and hopefully plant the seeds for a long-term rise. The formula calls for talent plus continuity plus dedication.

That's why Harvin's on-time arrival was key; why Peterson's improving health will be watched closely; and why Ponder's concern for Kalil — complete with chauffeur duties — had a certain charm.

"That's what is so exciting about this team," Ponder said. "We're so young. And a lot of us could be together for a long time."

A long time starts with three weeks in Mankato. ■

Adrian Peterson signed autographs for fans after arriving at training camp on July 26. JERRY HOLT, Star Tribune

Peterson's Back, But Not Back

All as his coach tried to temper the buzz, calling it just 'the next step.'

By MARK CRAIG/STAR TRIBUNE • August 12, 2012

MANKATO, MINN. — Vikings coach Leslie Frazier announced star running back Adrian Peterson's return to active duty with a smile and strong words of caution that couldn't have been more clear had they come with yellow flags and a giant banner screaming "Mission NOT Accomplished!"

"I want to caution you," Frazier said after Peterson was taken off the physically-unable-to-perform (PUP) list on Sunday morning. "I know there are a lot of fans that are very optimistic and excited about seeing him back. But for us, it's just a part of the process. It doesn't mean a whole lot other than he's done a great job in his rehab up to this point.

"He's done everything he can do on the side, and now it's the next step in the process. It doesn't mean in the future he's going to be lining up with our team in the opening game [against Jacksonville on Sept. 9]. We don't know that."

Now, whether fans and media choose to listen is, well, another matter. After all, the sight of the Vikings' four-time All-Pro taking a handoff from Christian Ponder during Sunday morning's walk-through was the most vivid indication that Peterson just might succeed in his quest to redefine the timetable for NFL players returning from the kind of devastating knee injury he suffered at Washington on Christmas Eve.

See. There we go. Looking too far ahead while wondering how a man made of flesh and bone — and a lot of muscle — has come this far in 7 1/2 months since his Dec. 30 surgery to repair torn anterior cruciate and medial collateral ligaments in his left knee.

That's OK. Someone else also was stirred by a routine walk-through.

"I was like a kid in a candy store today when I came out here and they threw me in with the first group," Peterson said. "I was smiling. I had to try to calm myself down. I was going a little too fast for a walk-through in the beginning. For me, this is so satisfying. I had a lot of people doubting me and saying this and saying that. But I kept my faith and kept working hard. Now, I'm back in the mix."

Per rules of the collective bargaining agreement, Peterson can't put full pads on until he's been through two practices. So he'll be limited to walk-throughs and individual drills until putting the pads on Tuesday. He also won't be tackled to the ground when the Vikings run their short-yardage and goal-line drills.

Peterson almost certainly won't play in Friday's second preseason game against the Buffalo Bills at Mall of America Field. A more likely target is the third preseason game against the San Diego Chargers a week from Friday at Mall of America Field. The fourth preseason game

at Houston is unlikely; teams typically rest most, if not all, of their starters in that game.

Peterson initially was told that his rehab would take nine months. But Frazier doesn't seem surprised that Peterson will be in pads before the second week of the preseason.

"Maybe if it were somebody else," Frazier said. "But with Adrian, he's unique and he's always been that way in the time I've known him in his career. He's special in so many ways."

But, again, Frazier tried to temper the perception that Peterson is all the way back. Going from pads to being game-ready and taking a hit is "a huge step," Frazier said.

"When you are in situations that aren't choreographed, to have to react will be a big step when that time comes," Frazier said. "Where guys can hit you anywhere, they can hit you low, they can hit you high. That's a big hurdle. Not just from a physical standpoint but from a mental one as well."

If you're one of those who may have doubted Peterson, he said you're not alone. He said he "sensed it" in some fans, media and, heck, even some of his family members.

"Some in the family weren't necessarily saying they're doubting [me], but they're not speaking the same words I'm speaking," Peterson said. "My vision, they're not seeing the same things. I know they love me and everything, but I'm in disagreement with them.

"It doesn't matter because I had my mind set on what I wanted to conquer. I knew it wasn't going to be easy. It was going to take work. I had my faith in the right place, my will in the right place. I'm back." ◼

Adrian Peterson at practice on August 12. CARLOS GONZALEZ, Star Tribune

Pads On, But Hands Off

Peterson practiced in full gear, but drills for the Vikings star are anything but full contact.

By DAN WIEDERER/STAR TRIBUNE • August 15, 2012

MANKATO, MINN. — On his first 11-on-11 handoff of his first training camp practice in pads Tuesday, Vikings running back Adrian Peterson burst through the line, slipped past a trio of linebackers and made it into the secondary untouched. Not a single defender even came close to putting a finger on him.

Of course, that was all by design.

Yes, Peterson's surgically repaired left knee seems to be nearing full strength again. And technically, he has been cleared to resume football activities in full. But until further notice, the Vikings have hung a giant "Do Not Touch" sign around Peterson's neck.

"The rules are simple," safety Jamarca Sanford said. "Do not touch 28. If you touch him, you're cut."

Coach Leslie Frazier admits he has had detailed discussions with his defense about handling the star running back with extreme care as Peterson blends back into practice. And just to make sure that message was clear, Frazier hopped into the defensive huddle just a moment before that first Peterson handoff to reiterate the orders.

"Now we have to adhere to it," Frazier said. "But one of the things they told me was, 'Coach, you know how he runs. What about protecting us?'"

Even as Peterson put on his pads Tuesday for the first time since December and giddily returned to work, it was obvious the Vikings aren't going to gamble much with him in practice.

Peterson did drill work as normal. But in 11-on-11 action, he was on the field for fewer than a dozen snaps. He took two handoffs, and both times defenders moved out of his way as if it were a family picnic and he was a 6-year-old owed a moment of glory.

Said Peterson: "Initially, I kind of expected to get hit or bumped or something. ... I'm still going to lower my shoulder. So those guys are probably going to get tired of touching off and tired of me putting my shoulder into them. They'll end up firing back."

Still, the tune accompanying the "Adrian Peterson Recovery Tour" has not changed. It's an orchestra of amazement, optimism and caution.

Frazier, his assistants and the medical staff continue to find themselves repeating the same motion -- that palms-down wave that says "Slow down." After all, it's been only 32 weeks and four days since Peterson came off the operating table with repaired anterior cruciate and medial collateral ligaments. So the baby-steps approach still is in use.

"[We're] just getting him increments along the way and not trying to bring it all back in one or two practices," Frazier said.

Meanwhile, Peterson still is vowing to be ready for the regular-season opener Sept. 9 and continues badgering the coaches for more work -- unsuccessfully, of course.

After that first handoff Tuesday, he received loud cheers from the fans.

"Oh, yeah! Standing ovation!" Sanford chided. "Standing ovation!"

And then after practice ended, Peterson took the podium for a brief, bright-lights news conference to recap his two-carry afternoon.

It was another sign of how important he is to the organization's future and a testament to the drive he's had to not miss a game in 2012.

"I had that vision," Peterson said. "I knew there would be a journey, a path to get closer to that vision. But I'm closer. I see it. It's closer now." ▪

Adrian Peterson at practice on August 14. JERRY HOLT, Star Tribune

Peterson Practicing Perfecting Patience

He'd prefer to play now, but understands why the Vikings want to be careful.

By DAN WIEDERER/STAR TRIBUNE • August 22, 2012

VIKINGS RUNNING BACK Adrian Peterson will not play in either of the team's final two preseason games, a decision coach Leslie Frazier confirmed Tuesday.

So now comes the logical next question: Is it a 100 percent certainty that Peterson will be on the field Sept. 9 when the regular season opens against Jacksonville?

"My goal is the same," Peterson said. "I want to be out there for that first game. So we'll see. That's where my mindset is. It hasn't changed at all. I'd be cheating myself if I said it was, uh, 95 percent [probable] or 85 percent. That's not the way I think."

If it were solely up to Peterson, he'd have put himself back in full-contact drills and exhibition games months ago. But the Vikings long ago wrestled such decisions away from their star running back, continuing to take the ultra-safe route.

To date, Peterson has done nothing but impress the coaches and medical staff with his recovery from knee surgery. Still, he returned to practice just last week, and the "Do Not Touch" rule Frazier established for Peterson has yet to be lifted.

Hence, the caution being shown in holding Peterson out of the preseason.

Over the next week and a half, the Vikings want to make certain they can test Peterson's instincts, quickness and comfort level in a controlled environment before exposing him to the high speeds of game action.

"Part of it," Frazier said, "is how he responds when some of the guys put a pad on him. How does he handle that? And when bodies fall down in front of him, how does he handle that? Does he stop and plant like the Adrian of old or does he just come to a standstill where he's [vulnerable] to taking a really serious hit?"

The official decision to hold Peterson out of the remaining two preseason games —Friday vs. the Chargers and Aug. 30 at Houston — was made Monday and Peterson responded with surprising acceptance.

"For the first time in our conversations, he kind of seemed like he understood," Frazier said. "He even used the word 'patience.' And I was like, 'Wow. Finally. It's clicking.' He's on board, everybody's on board. This is the right thing to do."

Peterson's eagerness to be back in action continues to percolate. And he admitted Tuesday that he's had difficulty trying to slow down.

"I've been preaching to myself," he said. "I've been repeating it and trying to brainwash myself. Patience. Patience. Because the past couple of weeks I really haven't

been hearing the things I've wanted to hear. So I've had to be patient."

Frazier said Peterson will be exposed to hitting in practice before he's thrown into game action. But the head coach had no timetable for exactly when that will occur.

Frazier also made a point to assert that holding Peterson back from preseason game action "doesn't guarantee he'll be ready for Jacksonville."

"But what it does," Frazier said, "is it gives us more time to throw more things at him in practice and get him prepared." ▪

Adrian Peterson works the ropes during the Vikings' training camp. JERRY HOLT, Star Tribune

Peterson Confident Coming Off Injury

By SID HARTMAN/STAR TRIBUNE • September 2, 2012

NOT MANY young football players suffer big injuries in their college and pro career the way Vikings star Adrian Peterson has. In 2006, he broke a collarbone his junior year at Oklahoma that forced him to miss the final seven regular-season games of his collegiate career, and now he is coming back from tearing two knee ligaments in the Vikings' second-to-last game of the 2011 season.

But the 27-year-old running back doesn't think he has been jinxed.

"No I don't think I'm jinxed at all," Peterson said. "That [first injury] happened my junior year. I'm five years in [the NFL]. That's a good span of time without having any serious injuries."

Looking back to his junior year in college when he came back from the collarbone injury for the Fiesta Bowl against Boise State, Peterson said he was not the least concerned about being injured again and believed he became a more aggressive player as a result.

Recalling the injury, he said: "It was against Iowa State, I was going to the end zone and I was going to reach in and dive to reach in, and the guy clipped my leg and my momentum changed and I landed right on my shoulder. I dug into the ground like a shovel on my left side. I felt it pop immediately."

Peterson missed three games last season after spraining his ankle against Oakland on Nov. 20. He returned in Week 14 against New Orleans but then tore the anterior cruciate and medial collateral ligaments in his left knee the following week at Washington after being tackled by safety DeJon Gomes on the first play of the second half. The injury ended what was another solid season for Peterson, who was averaging 4.7 yards per carry and finished 30 yards short of 1,000 rushing yards for the season.

Peterson feels like he can recover from his knee injury much like he did his shoulder injury, and come back a stronger player.

"I know that I'll be more aggressive coming off of this," he said. "Making sure that when guys try and go low on my leg, I'm going to be trying to run those guys over to keep them off my legs."

But he said there was no comparison in terms of the recovery process of this injury to his collarbone injury.

"For me, the upper body is easy for me to develop and you're still going to walk around," he said. "[The collarbone injury] kind of affected the way I slept a little bit. But when you talk about the ACL, you know, my muscles just shut down.

"I lost a lot of muscle in my leg. I couldn't walk. I couldn't do a lot. At least when I broke my collarbone, I could get up and go to the restroom when I wanted to. I couldn't do that with this injury. I couldn't walk up stairs for a long period of time. The pain is night and day."

He also had a dislocated shoulder as a freshman at Oklahoma and missed time as a sophomore because of a high ankle sprain, and it seemed like the injury concerns were a reason why he was still available when the Vikings took him seventh overall in the 2007 draft. As a pro, he missed two games during his sensational rookie season after injuring his right knee at Green Bay; the only other game he missed with the Vikings before last season was the 2010 game against Chicago at TCF Bank Stadium, when he was sidelined by a right thigh bruise.

Asked if he will be nervous when he carries the ball for the first time this season, he said: "I'm looking forward to getting my name called so I can suit up.

"Coming back? Yeah, probably anxiety will be there, excitement will be there. I'm going to try and stay within myself and not get caught up in the moment."

Adrian Peterson jokes with fellow running back Toby Gerhart during Vikings' training camp.
CARLOS GONZALEZ, Star Tribune

Play/Not Play Dilemma

Frazier's risk-reward decision about using Peterson in Week 1 is unusually complicated.

By DAN WIEDERER/STAR TRIBUNE • September 4, 2012

IF THE CALENDAR is correct, Sunday will be Sept. 9. Which is the Sunday of Week 1 in the NFL.

And Sept. 9 and Week 1, if memory serves, are the date and the event that have been rolling off Adrian Peterson's tongue just about every day since last January.

As in — and we're summarizing Peterson's talking points for the past eight months here — "I will be ready on Sept. 9. I will play in Week 1 against Jacksonville. That's the goal. I will reach that goal. And I won't let anyone stand in my way or tell me it's not possible."

So imagine the anxiety Vikings coach Leslie Frazier must be feeling this week. Sometime on Sunday morning, as the Vikings prepare to host the Jaguars in their 2012 season opener, Frazier will have to announce his final decision on whether Peterson can play.

On Sept. 9, in Week 1.

For Frazier, there will be nothing like starting a pivotal season with this kind of pressure and a call this big.

It's a decision that will either validate Peterson's comeback vows or temporarily deflate his morale.

Late last week, Frazier asserted he wouldn't make his final call until gameday, an assertion he stood by Monday.

What Frazier and the Vikings medical team want most is to put Peterson through a demanding week of practice. They want to evaluate how he responds as he continues to absorb some contact.

They want to see how instinctively he's moving and cutting and reacting on the fly. They want to gauge just how in tune he is with the game plan during an intense week of preparation.

Said Frazier: "We need to see him do some things physically within what we're trying to get done against Jacksonville."

And when it comes time Sunday to activate the traffic light — red, yellow or green — Frazier said he won't allow concern for Peterson's mood to influence the decision.

"You really have to take the emotion out of it," Frazier said. "You've got to really home in on what's best for him, what's best for our team. Adrian is not just another guy on our team. He is, in so many ways, the face of what we try to do. So we have to be able to see the big picture when it comes to him."

But aren't there fears that asking the star running back to take a seat on Sunday — on Sept. 9, in Week 1 — could send him into a funk, especially given how hard he's pushed and persevered and promised to be ready? Aren't there worries that Peterson, as eager and ambitious as he always is, won't be able to see that big picture himself?

"There was a point, maybe I would have worried about that," Frazier said Monday. "But of late, I think

he has really bought into some of the things we've been talking to him about from a preparation standpoint and how we want to approach this regular season."

On the one hand, the Vikings have to be ultra-careful with their star running back, taking into account that they aren't at this 2012 starting line stretching for a Super Bowl run.

The rebuilding process, like Peterson's recovery from major knee surgery, has to be approached with the right combination of urgency and patience. And every risk-reward scenario with Peterson points toward holding him back as long as possible, especially with Toby Gerhart more than capable of being an early-season workhorse.

On the other hand, the Vikings will also need to show serious signs of life in their four September games to keep an unsettled fan base from souring like three-week-old milk. Sunday's home date with the Jaguars is as winnable as any of those contests. And having Peterson in the mix, if only for a handful of touches, would send a jolt of energy through the Twin Cities and allow the enthusiastic running back to begin easing back toward a heavy workload.

Remember, this is a season where hope must quickly replace disgruntlement. And the ticking of the clock seems to have gotten louder this week. Now it'll be up to Frazier and the Vikings to make a major call on their offensive star. This one has a definitive deadline: Sept. 9, Week 1.

Adrian Peterson works out on Sept. 3. MATT GILMER, Star Tribune

He Meant What He Said

Peterson vowed he would be ready for Game 1. Now it's in the bosses' hands.

By DAN WIEDERER/STAR TRIBUNE • September 9, 2012

ON THURSDAY MORNING, with Vikings running back Adrian Peterson understanding his Week 1 status would be a game-time decision, he sat in an office at Winter Park still scheming to get his final say.

Moments earlier, during a 10-minute locker room exchange with reporters, Peterson sincerely professed his faith in Leslie Frazier's decision-making, vowing to accept whatever resolution the head coach reached.

But that didn't mean Peterson was above exerting pressure. So for a moment, he envisioned Sunday's pregame warmups and the pivotal verdict that would follow in the to-play-or-not-to-play saga.

"Oh yeah, I'm going to have a word in it. Believe that," Peterson said. "I will have my say."

Asked if it might take 10 people to pry his shoulder pads off, Peterson laughed.

"Probably a lot more than that."

Understand this: As the Vikings open the regular season Sunday against Jacksonville, Peterson has checked the box beside his biggest offseason goal.

Yes, he has always vowed to play in the season opener, virtually since the anesthesia wore off after his Dec. 30 surgery to repair torn anterior cruciate and medial collateral ligaments in his left knee.

But having himself ready to play with the decision now in the hands of Frazier and the front office counts for something, too.

"I feel like I've done everything I could do to be ready," Peterson said.

Peterson's goal to return to action on Sept. 9 still hangs in the balance.

Making good on a declaration that he will soon be better than ever before? Before long, Peterson will begin that next steep climb.

BACKFIELD BUDDIES

UNTIL FURTHER notice, Toby Gerhart will be the Vikings' workhorse back, the insurance policy that will allow Peterson to ease back into his groove.

Don't forget, it was Gerhart who uncorked the Vikings' longest run in 2011, a 67-yarder at Washington that came on the series after Peterson's gruesome season-ending knee injury.

Gerhart still laughs at his inability to reach the end zone on his big run, caught at the 8 by Redskins cornerback Josh Wilson.

"Around the 20, it felt like the whole field tilted uphill," Gerhart said.

But in rushing for 105 yards on nine carries after halftime that day and sparking a 33-26 victory, Gerhart added to the confidence he had been building throughout the second half of last season as his workload increased.

"I learned I can do this," he said. "With that confidence, you're able to relax and use your talents. You start seeing things earlier, hitting it faster."

Even Peterson has a profound admiration for Gerhart's

Adrian Peterson during training camp. JERRY HOLT, Star Tribune

dedication. The two backs, while competing for work, have developed a strong bond and an understanding that they can help each other. Peterson's eyes bug out when he talks of Gerhart's diligence in meetings, his penchant for asking good questions and thoroughly documenting everything that's being taught.

"I write things down," Peterson said. "But I don't write things down like Toby."

Gerhart speaks with similar amazement when noting Peterson's indefatigable drive. He thinks back to the Vikings' first session of organized team activities in May when Peterson, with his left knee still strengthening, spent much of the afternoon racing receiver Percy Harvin up the grassy hill beside the practice field.

"To see him competing stride for stride with Percy, to me, it left no doubts he was going to be back and as good as ever," Gerhart said.

Last week, Gerhart joined Peterson for a similar hill session, driven to keep up.

"It's not just his work ethic, it's his positivity," he said. "He's always at 100 miles per hour, pushing himself. But he never complains. You'll never hear him say, 'I'm sore. I'm tired. My legs feel heavy today.'"

WHAT COULD BE NEXT?

PETERSON HAS always embodied an enthusiasm to push forward. But now that eagerness has spiked, especially after an offseason that he acknowledges has been filled with a series of unusual and sometimes trying twists.

Of course there was all that grueling rehabilitation — the severe pain in the month after surgery followed by the incremental push to restore his range of motion, then his strength, then his ability to cut and react.

But there was off-the-field chaos as well. Peterson saw the back of a police car in July in Houston, arrested at a nightclub and charged with resisting arrest after a skirmish with security.

He also saw the back of an ambulance during training camp after a bizarre incident in which he had a seriously adverse reaction to cafeteria jambalaya.

"God has been testing me," Peterson said.

Neither episode has full closure. Peterson's next court date on the misdemeanor charge is scheduled for Sept. 27. He said he knows in his heart he committed no crime and never initiated contact with officers as the Houston Police Department alleges.

But Peterson will concede that he learned an important

JEFF WHEELER, Star Tribune

lesson from that incident, admitting he probably inflamed things with one last acerbic comment on the way out the door.

"I saw how fast something can flip, just like that," Peterson said. "So innocent. It wasn't meant to get to that level. So I've been able to step back and get a different view of Adrian and things I need to be better about. ... You need to know when to walk away.

"Yeah, I've got the freedom of speech to say what I want to say. But me saying what I wanted to say added to what happened. I'm not saying you submit to anyone. But I could have cut it short."

Peterson is also still awaiting results back on the exam he underwent to test for food allergies. His fingers are crossed it wasn't seafood that sent him to the hospital in Mankato.

"That's all I eat is seafood," Peterson said. "I probably ate over 60 pounds of crawfish this offseason. Crab legs, stone crab, blue crab, Dungeness crabs. I can't go without seafood."

'I'M BACK'

PETERSON'S RETURN to action will inevitably feature additional obstacles to maneuver around. Yet while many athletes recovering from ACL tears experience a dip in confidence and a bit of hesitance in their injured knee, Peterson has no such worries. Neither do the people around him.

"Adrian doesn't understand hesitance," Gerhart said. "But I don't think you can. The moment you slow down and start playing cautious is the moment you get rolled on. Adrian's going to attack this and play like nothing was ever wrong."

Added running backs coach James Saxon: "That desire and that positive demeanor is who Adrian is and how he's made. I don't know if anybody can accurately give you the answers of what and why and when and how with how far he's come. But I told him to go hug his mom and dad for passing on that DNA and that mindset."

Peterson's first carry — whether it comes in Week 1 or Week 2 — will be a symbolic milestone, a testament to his resolve, ambition and contagious positive energy.

So how will Peterson himself know he's back? Like fully back, All-Pro caliber again.

Not surprisingly, it's a question the Vikings star answers with little hesitation.

"I know already on the inside that I'm back," he said. "It's about me getting out there now and making it known." ∎

JEFF WHEELER, Star Tribune

Shiny Pair of Boots

Walsh, Peterson, Ponder take away boost of confidence with first win.

By DAN WIEDERER/STAR TRIBUNE • September 10, 2012

THE OFFICIAL attendance for the Vikings' opener Sunday: 56,607. Which means at least 50,000 people wandered into downtown Minneapolis in the late afternoon still in a daze and struggling to comprehend what all had happened.

Some left prematurely, shortly after Jacksonville receiver Cecil Shorts hauled in a 39-yard touchdown pass from Blaine Gabbert with 20 seconds left. After the two-point conversion, the Jaguars led 23-20 and the most impatient and cynical Vikings fans stomped out of Mall of America Field wondering why that bitter 2011 aftertaste was still lingering.

Another blown lead late?

Another home loss?

Was this yet another example of a bad team finding a new agonizing way to lose?

But then something crazy happened. Many things actually. And after Sunday's final play — a wobbly Gabbert incompletion in overtime — the Vikings had somehow stolen a 26-23 victory.

Just like that, a wave of euphoria washed away most of the displeasure.

It was that kind of unbelievable afternoon. So unbelievable, in fact, that the Vikings' final 12 points came off the foot of their rookie kicker, Blair Walsh, a calm and confident 22-year-old whose selection in the sixth round of April's draft raised a few eyebrows at the time.

But Walsh absolutely crunched a 55-yard tying field goal on the final play of regulation, then completed his perfect afternoon with a 38-yard field goal on the Vikings' first possession of overtime.

"His intestinal fortitude is incredible," coach Leslie Frazier said.

Added defensive end Brian Robison: "First NFL game. Rookie kicker. Game-winner. Game-tying kick. In my mind, he should definitely get a game ball."

And probably more than that.

Sunday's victory was so unbelievable that 48 hours after the Vikings finished their final practice of Week 1 insisting Adrian Peterson's availability would be a game-time decision, the eager running back wound up taking 17 carries, rushing for 84 yards and scoring both Vikings touchdowns.

Peterson was asked whether that sizable workload was more than he expected.

"It was less," he said, not kidding even a little. "I was ready to carry the load."

Later, Peterson was asked if he could handle even more work next week.

"Yeah. I'm feeling good right now," he responded. "My legs are loose. Seriously."

Really? The franchise running back is already feeling back to normal and producing like his old self barely eight months removed from major knee surgery? Yep, unbelievable.

Things were so unbelievable Sunday that Christian

Adrian Peterson sprints away from Jaguar Paul Posluszny during a 19-yard run in the third quarter.
BRIAN PETERSON, Star Tribune

Ponder shook off an inexplicably lethargic start by the offense to deliver the biggest drive of his young pro career with little time and no margin for error.

It was a two-play march that required only 10 seconds. Ponder completed passes of 26 and 6 yards to Devin Aromashodu and Kyle Rudolph, respectively. And that put Walsh in position for the tying bomb as regulation ended.

"Even before we had to go out there," Ponder said, "I was telling guys that we're going to need our two-minute offense. I don't know that guys believed me. But I told them we had to stay in it. Fortunately they did and we were focused."

The Vikings made good on a handful of offseason promises during the opener. They promised Ponder would be better in Year 2. And after the Vikings dry-heaved their way to four punts on their first four possessions, Ponder responded by going 17-for-20 for 238 yards the rest of the way.

Six completions went to Percy Harvin for 84 yards, five to Kyle Rudolph for 67 more yards.

Peterson had promised since January that he had play in the opener. And he delivered, sending a jolt of energy through the Metrodome first with his introduction in the starting lineup and later by showing that brilliant burst-and-blast running style of his.

His longest run was a 20-yarder in overtime, allowing him to break Robert Smith's franchise career rushing record.

Said Frazier: "Some of those runs, I told Adrian afterward, 'I'm not sure you weren't just faking that ACL [injury].'"

That's not to say Sunday's victory was a masterpiece. Not by any stretch. There were the early defensive struggles, with Jacksonville delivering scoring drives of 17 plays and 77 yards and 11 plays and 78 yards early on.

There were silly penalties throughout.

And there was Shorts' TD grab in the closing seconds of regulation, with cornerback Chris Cook in coverage and unable to spin and locate the ball.

In a league defined by dramatic mood swings, a galling loss Sunday could have sent this mostly young, mostly unproven bunch staggering for quite a while.

Instead, a gutty rally and an improbable victory provided what the Vikings promised to deliver throughout 2012: resolve, toughness, rays of hope. ∎

Adrian Peterson celebrated a three-yard touchdown in the second quarter against Jacksonville. ELIZABETH FLORES, Star Tribune

What a Rush to See AP Good as His Word

He said he would be healthy. His two TDs and 84 yards were convincing evidence.

By JIM SOUHAN/STAR TRIBUNE • September 2, 2012

IF ADRIAN PETERSON sends you an e-mail asking for money, claiming he's a prince from a foreign land with a once-in-a-lifetime deal, cut him a check.

If he tells you eating 18 grapefruits a day will help you lose 20 pounds, rent a refrigerated truck and drive to Florida.

In a league overflowing with disinformation, Peterson's word, from now on, is bullion. He earned the Better Business Bureau stamp of approval and his teammates' awe on Sunday, leading the Vikings to a victory as improbable and timely as his comeback.

Eight months after shredding his knee in a meaningless game in Washington, D.C., Peterson proved his vows to play in the Vikings opener were neither wishful thinking nor an unhealthy obsession, carrying 17 times for 84 yards and two touchdowns in the Vikings' 26-23 overtime victory over Jacksonville.

Peterson promised this all along, but the Vikings, citing the severity of his injury, sowed doubt. Vikings coach Leslie Frazier admitted Sunday afternoon that Peterson moved so well in practice that he held him out of preseason games not to preserve his health but because he had little to prove.

"We thought 10 to 15 carries would be great," Frazier said. "He wound up with 17, which is just about where we wanted him to be.

"After some of those runs, I said, 'I'm not sure you weren't just faking that ACL.' He looked pretty good to me."

A recently mended anterior cruciate ligament couldn't keep Peterson from breaking the franchise records for rushing yards. He has 6,836, — 18 more than Robert Smith, whose taped tribute appeared on the scoreboard, with Smith urging Peterson to pursue the "other" Smith, Emmitt, who holds the NFL record with 18,355 yards.

That record, of course, is out of reach.

Unless Peterson says it isn't.

"I pretty much knew that I'd be out playing today, but I had to keep it under wraps," Peterson said.

He bolted for 20 yards on one run. On the other 16, he took the kind of beating that would have caused cringing on the Vikings sideline had they not believed he was fully healed.

"As the game went on, you asked him how he's doing and he's giving you a response," Frazier said. "We talked

Adrian Peterson takes the field for the season opener. JERRY HOLT, Star Tribune

about him being completely honest and not having any pride about if anything was bothering him, and we would pull him if we had to.

"It did encourage me, once we saw how he was handling things. Then we thought he could do a little more as the game went on."

The Vikings called 28 designed runs; Peterson carried on 17 of them. He caught one pass for 3 yards and, when the Vikings used him as a decoy in an ill-fated series near the Jaguars goal line in the fourth quarter, he gestured to the bench and sprinted off in frustration.

He carried more often than anyone could have expected, and less than he would have liked. "It was less," he said. "I was expecting to carry the load. I understand from their perspective how they're looking at it, but from my perspective, I knew I would be ready to play. It's a great way to start the season."

We've always marveled at his conditioning and competitiveness. "And his genetics," Frazier said.

What Peterson proved over the past eight months is that he's just as spectacular grinding through a morning workout in the spring as he is stiff-arming a linebacker in the fall.

We knew he could defy gravity and inertia. We didn't know, until Sunday, that he could ignore medical history and conventional wisdom.

He got hurt playing in a meaningless game for a bad team, and he pushed himself for eight months to play in a game that could prove meaningless against a mediocre opponent at the beginning of a rebuilding season.

We're accustomed to athletes protecting their futures, their earning power.

What Peterson did Sunday, and has done for the past eight months, spoke of athletic bravery.

"It feels amazing," he said.

He should have seen how it looked. ▪

ELIZABETH FLORES, Star Tribune

Despite Strong Debut, Peterson Says Best to Come

By MARK CRAIG/STAR TRIBUNE • September 14, 2012

WE'VE LEARNED that whatever Adrian Peterson says is pretty much exactly how it is. For eight months, the Vikings running back said he'd play in the season opener and eventually be back as good if not better than he as he was before. Then he carried the ball 17 times for 84 yards and two touchdowns in Sunday's 26-23 season-opening win over the Jaguars.

So the assumption now would be that Peterson met his goal of being as good if not better than he was before.

Peterson says that's wrong. He says he's "95 percent" of what he was before. The other 5 percent is "just being more explosive with my strength."

"It don't sound like much from the outside looking in, but I know my game and I know where I want to be," Peterson said. "And it's going to be huge once I get 100 percent. Like night and day. Seriously. I'm just keeping that in mind." ■

JERRY HOLT, Star Tribune

Peterson Gleefully Defies Odds in Recovery

His performance against Jaguars was mind-boggling — even by running back's outsized standards.

By DAN WIEDERER/STAR TRIBUNE • September 16, 2012

ONLY FOUR SECONDS remained last Sunday when Blair Walsh trotted onto Mall of America Field for the first high-pressure kick of his NFL career.

The Vikings trailed Jacksonville 23-20 after surrendering a demoralizing late touchdown.

Walsh faced a 55-yard game-tying kick, longer than all but one of the field goals he made during his four years at Georgia. The adrenaline and anxiety were quickly elevating.

Until Adrian Peterson approached on his way off the field, offering an encouraging bop to Walsh's head, a thump so forceful it actually turned the kicker's helmet a few inches.

Walsh's first thought: "Wow, that's ridiculous."

The rookie's startled laugh broke the tension. He made the kick with ease.

"I don't think Adrian knows how strong he is," Walsh said.

Yep, sources have confirmed it. Peterson continues redefining ridiculous. And nope, he doesn't seem to know his own strength.

A week ago we were wondering whether he would even play against the Jaguars, just a little more than eight months after he underwent major surgery on his left knee. Now, with the Vikings in Indianapolis, we're wondering whether Peterson is already set to take on a full workload.

Maybe a 22-, 23-carry day?

Seems hopeful. But don't rule anything out.

Not with the way Peterson ran a week ago, using his confidence and self-professed faith to run right past the hesitation that should be slowing him down right now.

Now the question must be asked: Will Peterson's rapid recuperation be a source of inspiration for a team trying to prove it can accomplish more than a huge legion of outside doubters believe?

Or will Peterson's extraordinary progress skew the realistic view for how quickly dramatic upturns can occur?

After all, for months Vikings fans have been lectured to have patience with this young squad, reminded that after a season as frustrating and failure-filled as last year's, remarkable recoveries just don't happen in the blink of an eye.

Except when they do.

Last week, Peterson delivered 17 carries for 84 yards

JERRY HOLT, Star Tribune

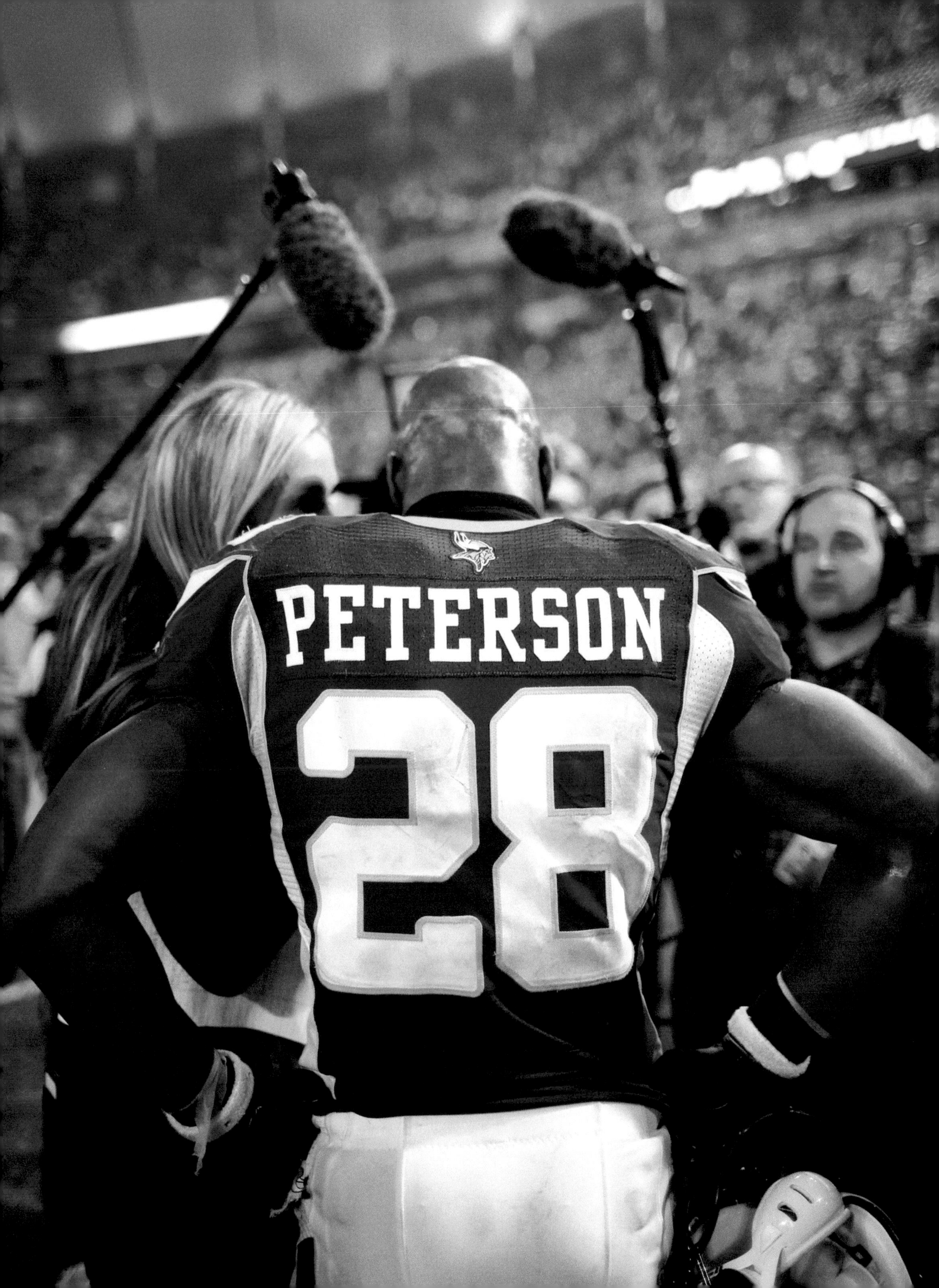
PETERSON
28

with two touchdowns. And had receiver Stephen Burton held his block just a second longer on Peterson's longest run of the day, a 20-yarder in overtime, the chaos at the Metrodome may have culminated with a 62-yard game-ending touchdown run.

"It was real close," Peterson said.

Which means Peterson was real close to having himself a 130-yard, three-TD day. In his first game back after ACL surgery.

Colts coach Chuck Pagano has watched the film of the Vikings' opener and sees little difference between the Peterson of last week and the one who chewed him up for 166 yards from scrimmage in 2009 when Pagano was defensive coordinator in Baltimore.

"He's a superhuman guy," Pagano said. "Just a rare, rare, rare talent."

Pagano was particularly impressed with Peterson's first touchdown run, a 3-yarder that required an instinctive and sharp cut back left.

On the Vikings' next drive, Peterson scored again, launching himself into the end zone from the 3, then quickly doing a back somersault to pop to his feet.

Yes, Peterson experienced some minor soreness and tightness in his knee after the game. But, he said, that was to be expected. He also believes he's only operating at about 95 percent right now.

So just what is missing in that final 5 percent?

"Just being more explosive with my strength," Peterson said. "It doesn't sound like much from the outside looking in. But I know my game and I know where I want to be. And it's going to be huge once I get to 100 percent. Like night and day. Seriously."

Most refreshing? With every reason to be boastful, Peterson hasn't launched a vain "Look at me" campaign. Instead, he's simply asked outsiders to understand the unwavering self-belief he's used in his comeback.

"I had my vision, I knew what I wanted to do, and that's all that matters," he said.

Ridiculous. Guy doesn't know his own strength. ■

Peterson in pregame against the Jaguars.
JEFF WHEELER, Star Tribune

First 100-Yard Game

Peterson feels 'icy,' cools off Lions with 102-yard outburst.

By DAN WIEDERER/STAR TRIBUNE • October 1, 2012

DETROIT — Adrian Peterson sure seemed to have his trademark burst back Sunday. The Vikings running back asserted earlier in the week that a bruising 25-carry, 86-yard day in Week 3 against San Francisco had been like a can of WD-40, removing those last flecks of rust away from his game.

Then in Sunday's surprising 20-13 upset of Detroit at Ford Field, Peterson appeared to be his old self again. Rushing for 102 yards on 21 carries, he gave the Vikings just what they needed in the ground game, notching his 28th career 100-yard day and the first since a home loss to Green Bay last October.

Before the game, Peterson felt a big day coming on and told receiver Percy Harvin that he was feeling "icy."

"When he tells me icy, that means he's smooth and ready to go," Harvin said.

Peterson's first carry went for 12 yards. He later added big gains of 18 and 10 yards and picked up a first down on one run on which he had his shoe ripped by Lions defensive end Cliff Avril but kept fighting for yards.

Not surprisingly, the postgame Peterson praise was flowing.

"That guy's a beast, man," said receiver Jerome Simpson. "You've got to get him touches and he's going to make a play."

Added Avril: "Can't take anything from that guy. He's a heck of a football player." ▪

Adrian Peterson avoids the Lions' Justin Durant. JERRY HOLT, Star Tribune

Peterson's Road Back Has Come Full Circle

Now he returns, back in one piece and as confident as ever.

By JIM SOUHAN/STAR TRIBUNE • October 12, 2012

THE LAST TIME Adrian Peterson visited FedEx Field in Landover, Md., he writhed on the turf, as other players knelt and prayed. He rode the medical cart off the field, knowing there was a "99.9" percent chance he had torn ligaments in his left knee.

He sat in the locker room, hearing cheers as distant echoes, already anticipating months of tedious recovery.

On Dec. 24, 2011, at the lowest point of his professional career, Adrian Peterson called over Jeff Anderson, the Vikings director of corporate communications.

Peterson had noticed a kid wearing his jersey behind the bench. The kid, Keenan Wynn, had hung a banner listing Peterson's autograph as one of his Christmas wishes.

"Mr. Anderson came out in the fourth quarter and said, 'Excuse me, do you mind if I borrow that jersey for a moment?'" said Dr. Michael Wright, who mentors Wynn.

Peterson autographed the jersey, wishing Wynn, "Merry Christmas."

"I started to tear up," Wright said. "I know a lot of the athletes, and that moment made me feel like a kid again. Never had a player of that caliber, at a time when he was injured and worried that he may never play again, think of doing something so generous."

Peterson keeps giving, in so many ways.

Refusing to accept the logical and conservative timetables that would have had him easing his way into the season following his knee surgery, Peterson has rushed 96 times for 420 yards in five games. "I have the drive to be the best ever to play," he said Thursday. "I couldn't just go through the motions. I had a fire burning in me."

Ten months after an injury that may have slowed a lesser athlete, Peterson is eying another decade in the league, noting that a certain Redskins linebacker has lasted. "London Fletcher is 37," Peterson said. "I'm 27. That's 10 more years. I feel like I can go for a long time. There's a lot you can do with your body when you're well-conditioned. Herschel Walker, today, I'm sure he's benching over 400 pounds and they say he just ran a 4.4 or 4.3 40."

Buoyed by his team's 4-1 start and Percy Harvin's transformation from versatile oddity to star, Peterson calls himself and Harvin the two best players in the league. "I know talent," he said. "I can watch Michael Jordan and Scottie Pippen and see the difference."

Who's Pippen and who's Jordan? "There are two Jordans on this team," he said. "I'm not trying to be cocky. I'm just very confident in my abilities."

And Harvin's. He remembered watching the national championship game in January 2009, when Harvin played with a hairline fracture in his ankle yet looked like the best player on the field as his Florida Gators beat Oklahoma. "I watched that game, and I knew he was a star," Peterson said. "When he came out in the draft, I

knew there was a chance for him to drop to us."

The Vikings once landed Randy Moss with the 21st pick in the 1998 draft. Because of injury concerns, Peterson fell to them at No. 7 in 2007. They landed Harvin with the 22nd pick in 2009.

"The way they evaluate talent here, I knew we wouldn't pass on him," Peterson said. "They didn't pass on me. Those three names right there -- c'mon, how are those guys not taken in the top five?

"Percy is the best player I've ever played with."

Peterson's return to FedEx Field is one of the prominent NFL story lines this week. He shrugs off the memories as if they were arm tackles. "I was in disbelief," he said. "But by the time we took the flight back, I was thinking about rehabbing it. I turned the page."

But not before leaving a Christmas present for someone he had never met.

"That was a life-changing experience for Keenan," Wright said. "He has Mr. Peterson's jersey hanging now. He's doing better in school and he's excellent in sports.

"When Keenan wanted to meet Adrian, I told him, 'If you believe in something bad enough, it will happen.' Mr. Peterson made it happen."

Adrian Peterson takes the field at Washington. JERRY HOLT, Star Tribune

Peterson Experiences Emotionally Charged Day

By DAN WIEDERER/STAR TRIBUNE • October 15, 2012

LANDOVER, MD. — Adrian Peterson had mixed feelings Sunday when he returned to FedEx Field. The Vikings running back severely injured his left knee there last Christmas Eve and had flashbacks to that career-altering moment.

"There was a little emotion," he said. "But I was able to overpower that with the main focus of trying to get out there and win."

Peterson, despite a tender left ankle, opened the day by rushing for 40 yards on the Vikings' opening field goal drive in a 38-26 loss to Washington. That included a shifty 32-yard run. Peterson also had a heated face-mask-to-facemask argument with Redskins cornerback DeAngelo Hall in the first quarter.

"He slapped me in the face after making a good tackle," Peterson said. "And I was just telling him, 'Hey, don't do me like that, brother.' I looked him in the eyes and he knew I meant business."

Peterson finished with 17 carries for 79 yards and added a career-best seven catches for 50 yards. But his scoreless streak reached five games when his 1-yard touchdown run with 32 seconds left was negated by Kyle Rudolph's false start.

Peterson also expressed disappointment in himself, saying he missed some early opportunities to break free.

"I missed a couple [holes]," he said. "Should have been more aggressive. That's pretty much what it boils down to."

Adrian Peterson breaks a tackle against Washington. BRIAN PETERSON, Star Tribune

Peterson Picks up Slack

The running back didn't play like someone with a sore ankle.

By MARK CRAIG/STAR TRIBUNE • October 22, 2012

IT MIGHT BE a quarterback's league, but a running back walked out of Mall of America Field with Vikings owner Zygi Wilf's purple tie Sunday.

"Pretty nice, huh?" asked Adrian Peterson, showing Vikings General Manager Rick Spielman the trophy Wilf occasionally passes out to a star player after a victory.

Seconds later, Peterson explained why he thinks the Vikings can be a Super Bowl contender after an offensively ugly 21-14 victory over Arizona.

"We have shown that we can be productive in the run game and the pass game," Peterson said. "Obviously, [quarterback] Christian [Ponder] didn't play as well as he would have liked and as well as we would have liked today. But you have those games. That's why we're a team."

Ponder had the worst passer rating (35.5) of any game he's started and finished in his two-year career. But Peterson had another benchmark game against Arizona. A year after he ran for 122 yards and three touchdowns on 29 carries, Peterson faced a steady dose of eight- and nine-man fronts and still crushed the Cardinals again with 153 yards and one touchdown on 23 carries (6.7). Throw in 6 more yards on two receptions, and Peterson accounted for 76.1 percent of the team's 209 yards of offense. Not bad for a guy with a tender ankle.

"It's just nice to rely on other guys to take over the game for you," Ponder said. "Obviously, Adrian did that today. It definitely takes pressure off of me as a quarterback."

A week ago, Peterson lamented his lack of aggression as the Vikings settled for three field goals in three first-quarter red-zone trips en route to a loss at Washington. Peterson changed that on the Vikings' first red-zone play against the Cardinals.

On first-and-10 from the Arizona 13, Peterson took a handoff left, cut back to the middle and shot through a hole. He slammed through safeties Adrian Wilson and James Sanders inside the 5-yard line and reached the ball across the goal line with his right hand for a 7-0 lead with 8 minutes, 46 seconds left in the opening quarter. On the day, the Vikings went 2-for-2 on touchdowns in the red zone after going 2-for-7 a week ago.

Peterson had 92 yards rushing in the first half. With 6:08 left in the third quarter, he broke off a 22-yard run to surpass 100 yards. And his final carry, an 8-yard explosion on fourth-and-5 with 14 seconds left, ended the game.

"I feel like I [changed my mentality]," Peterson said. "That carried the guys. Up front [on the line], the fullbacks, the receivers, they were really out there being aggressive. That's the type of football we want to play."

Naturally, after the game, there was another round of questions about whether Peterson is 100 percent back from the left knee reconstruction he had done last December.

"Well," said receiver Percy Harvin, "If he's not 100, I'd say he's 99.8."

And he's got the purple tie to prove it. ◼

Adrian Peterson scores a first-quarter touchdown against Arizona. CARLOS GONZALEZ, Star Tribune

All Day's Big Day a Big Waste

Peterson rushed for 182 yards and two TDs.

By MARK CRAIG/STAR TRIBUNE • November 5, 2012

SEATTLE — Yes, the Vikings lost a game on the fourth-most productive day of Adrian Peterson's stellar career.

Yes, they lost by double digits on an afternoon when Peterson averaged 10.7 yards per carry, the second-highest total he has ever had. And, yes, they lost 30-20 to the Seahawks at CenturyLink Stadium with the league's leading rusher exploding for the second-longest carry of his career — 74 yards to the 1-yard line — on the second snap of the game against the league's fifth-ranked run defense.

"It's a problem, man," Peterson said when asked if he was surprised to lose on a day when the Vikings ran for 243 yards and two touchdowns on 27 carries (9.0). "We've got to have more big plays."

That was the general mood in the locker room as the Vikings complimented Peterson on another amazing game while lamenting a mere 44 net yards passing in a loss that dropped them to 5-4.

"It's tough," quarterback Christian Ponder said. "We have to piggyback off those when Adrian has a great game."

Peterson pointed the finger at himself first, saying that he could have scored a touchdown on a play in which he slipped and fell in the backfield. But it's safe to say that 182 yards and two touchdowns on 17 carries — and 193 total yards from scrimmage — was a job well done for Peterson, who has 957 yards rushing in only nine games since having his left knee reconstructed.

While Ponder was compiling a 37.3 passer rating, Seattle rookie Russell Wilson was posting a 127.3 rating with three touchdowns, no interceptions and only one sack.

In other words, the rookie took advantage of the league's second-leading rusher, Marshawn Lynch, running for 124 yards and a touchdown on 26 carries (4.8).

As a team, the Seahawks finished with 195 yards on 45 carries (4.3), including 128 yards on 28 second-half carries.

The Vikings ran the ball only nine times for 46 yards in the second half. Strangely, Peterson had only five carries for 38 yards after halftime.

"It's a little frustrating," Peterson said. "You just see what you can do and see how you can improve and go from there. That's going to be our focus point. Establish the run and try to be more productive in the pass game. It's obvious we didn't have a big game passing.

"Forty-four yards, it's hard to win like that, and we still could have. That's the scary thing. So once we get that corrected. I've got a lot of faith in Christian."

Besides the 74-yarder, Peterson had runs of 24, 16, 15 and 11 yards. After the 15-yarder, safety Earl Thomas drew Peterson's ire by celebrating the tackle.

"I was surprised," Peterson said. "I got up and he was celebrating like he had just won the lottery or something. I was shocked. I was just looking at him like, 'What are you celebrating for?'"

It was that kind of day. A lot of big runs for Peterson, but a lot more celebrating for the Seahawks. ▪

Adrian Peterson takes off on a 74-yard run against Seattle. MCKENNA EWEN, Star Tribune

Full Speed Ahead

Peterson wowed everyone and the defense racked up sacks and takeaways.

By DAN WIEDERER/STAR TRIBUNE • November 12, 2012

EVERYWHERE you looked the euphoria spread.

Following Sunday's 34-24 victory over Detroit at Mall of America Field, just about everybody within the Vikings organization had the look of a theme park mascot, their grins wide, bright and seemingly permanent.

Coach Leslie Frazier took the podium, beaming because his team had again proven resilient, undeterred by a two-game losing streak that stirred up a hurricane of outside negativity.

Instead of drowning under the crashing waves of criticism, the Vikings convinced themselves they were better than Detroit, then proved it with enough big plays to offset their sloppy lapses.

Rookie receiver Jarius Wright? His smile was one of eagerness. After waiting until Week 10 just to be active for the first time — a promotion that came because Percy Harvin couldn't play on his sprained ankle — Wright made an immediate impact. On his first series, he delivered a 54-yard reception and a 3-yard TD catch.

Never mind that during rehearsal for that deep pass Friday, Wright dropped the ball, a mistake he admits shook him.

"I was like, 'I can't miss my moment,'" he said.

When the lights came on, he didn't.

Of course, the Vikings took their biggest smiles Sunday from the play of Adrian Peterson, who might be having the most remarkable season of any player in the NFL right now.

For the fourth consecutive game, Peterson topped 100 yards rushing, this time racking up 171 on 27 carries.

No run was bigger than his 61-yard touchdown explosion with 8:06 left, the insurance score the Vikings so badly needed, providing a 31-17 lead as Detroit fueled up for one of its trademarked fourth-quarter rallies.

To that end, Peterson played the role of closer, touching the ball on nine of the Vikings' first 12 fourth-quarter snaps and aiding three consecutive scoring drives.

The Lions' comeback was not to be.

Peterson's is only picking up steam.

The running back's impressive surge — he has 629 yards over the past four games — now comes with a frightening promise.

"I'm going to come back stronger and better after the bye," Peterson vowed.

If losses to Tampa Bay and Seattle produced major questions about the strength of the run defense and the mercurial confidence of quarterback Christian Ponder, the only doubt to surface Sunday surrounded whether Peterson really had major knee surgery in December.

"I'm not totally sure if he did or not," left guard Charlie Johnson joked. "I'd like to think we do our job up front to spring him. But there are so many times he makes us look good. The guy's amazing."

With Harvin out, Peterson's big day proved timely. But Sunday's victory was far from a one-man show.

So many players provided big plays. Such as Chad Greenway's first-quarter interception, a pass he tore out of tight end Brandon Pettigrew's hands. That enabled the Vikings to steal three points, even with an ensuing offensive series that lost 5 yards.

There were also the nine receivers Ponder completed

passes to. That came as part of a 24-for-32, 221-yard, two-TD effort.

All last week, Frazier promised that there would be adjustments to the offense — to protections, to routes, to play calls.

Sunday, those tweaks led to a season-best 34 points.

"The key," Frazier said, "is Christian being able to go through his progressions. If something was taken away, go to the next guy. Be patient in the pocket. Deliver the ball on target."

To that end, Ponder was solid. Yes, there was that early deep strike and TD toss to Wright. But more important, there was also the revival of the Ponder-to-Kyle Rudolph connection, good for seven completions and 64 yards, including a 20-yard score.

Some pregame words of wisdom from quarterbacks coach Craig Johnson seemed to calm Ponder.

"Coach Johnson talked about just going out and playing without worrying about the consequences of your throws," he said. "Go out and let 'er rip. That's what I did."

Afterward, the good vibrations were everywhere, with Charlie Johnson providing the most fitting explanation.

In Week 11, the Vikings will be on bye, giving them two full weeks to absorb Sunday's result. A double-digit victory certainly provided a lot more peace of mind than a third consecutive loss would have.

"This will help guys relax more," Johnson said. "If we had lost this, going into the bye with three straight losses, that's a lot of time to be thinking and trying to figure stuff out. ... You can never relax in this league. But [with a win like this], you can take a deep breath with the understanding that when we do play, we can play pretty well." ▪

Adrian Peterson eluded the final Lions defender, Ricardo Silva, on a 61-yard touchdown run in the fourth quarter. JEFF WHEELER, Star Tribune

Enjoy It, Minnesotans, Greatness Is In Our Midst

By JIM SOUHAN/STAR TRIBUNE • November 12, 2012

MINNESOTANS have watched Hall of Famers play for the Twins and Vikings, and a future Hall of Famer play for the Timberwolves. At a few brief moments in time, they could claim to be watching the best player in the world. Never could they be so sure as they are today.

Adrian Peterson is the best football player in the world.

He may not be the most important, not in a sport ruled by quarterbacks.

He may be surpassed at any time, in the Darwinian league in which he plays.

If the measures of a complete football player are strength, speed, quickness, toughness, agility, resilience, competitiveness and production, Peterson is at the moment unmatched.

He's becoming the player of the year when he should have been thrilled with being considered the comeback player of the year.

"I can still get stronger," he said. "I'm still not there, man."

We can agree to disagree. He might be the most dominant athlete in modern Minnesota sports history.

When basketball was in its infancy, George Mikan might have been the best in the game. Kevin Garnett could have argued, for a year or two, that he was the world's best all-around basketball player. Kirby Puckett might

have risen to the top of baseball's ranks for a few months. Johan Santana and Frank Viola were the best once-every-five-days employees in baseball during their primes.

Nobody in Minnesota history has ever done what Peterson is doing: Dominating the most brutal and popular sport in the country less than a year after undergoing reconstructive knee surgery.

Sunday, his team took a 17-10 lead into the fourth quarter as his team tried to fend off a Lions rally that would have left the Vikings with a three-game losing streak.

In the fourth quarter, Peterson carried 11 times for 120 yards and a touchdown, plus a two-point conversion. For the game, he rushed 27 times for 171 yards. For the season, he has rushed 195 times for 1,128 yards and seven touchdowns, and a per-carry average of 5.8, the highest rate of his career. He's caught 29 passes for 155 yards, already the third-highest reception total of his career.

He set a team record for most yards rushing in the first 10 games of a season, and most rushing yards in a game against Detroit, and most rushing yards in three consecutive games (476). He leads the NFL in rushing yards and fan gasps. To twist an old line, he's saying goodbye to defenders when they thought it was time for them to say hello.

His teammates rave, of course.

Kevin Williams said Peterson has come back from his injury more patient, more willing to wait for blocks and slither up the middle for hidden yardage. "I think he's matured in that way," Williams said.

Christian Ponder knows Peterson is headed for a long run when he sees Peterson's body lean, like a downhill skier fighting through a turn. "I can tell after the first 10 yards or so and I can see his body angle down, and he takes off," Ponder said.

Peterson said he's even hearing praise from his most grudging critics — opposing defenders. "They just tell me that, 'You're great, just some of the things you're doing,'" Peterson said. "I guess it shocked me. You're out there, you're playing against guys and they come up and say different things like that to you."

Peterson said he was "humbled." His coach doesn't doubt that.

"The thing that sticks out to me about Adrian when you talk about superstars is his humility," Leslie Frazier said. "He may be the most humble superstar I've ever been around, and I've been around some great ones."

Ponder played well on Sunday, but it was Peterson who closed like Mariano Rivera. The Vikings led 24-17 when they took the ball on their 25 with 9:13 remaining. Peterson burst left for 19. On the next play, he burst right, and Ponder saw Peterson's body lean left like a stock car, and he sprinted 61 yards for the touchdown that allowed the Vikings to exhale.

"I'm definitely going to be working out during the bye week," Peterson said. "It's not a week off for me. I'm going to come back stronger and better."

Of course he is. ▪

Adrian Peterson leaves the field after the Vikings beat Detroit at the Metrodome. JERRY HOLT, Star Tribune

AP for MVP? Stats Make a Strong Case

By MARK CRAIG/STAR TRIBUNE • November 14, 2012

HERE WERE Barry Sanders' rushing totals through 10 games in 1997, the year he ran for 2,053 yards and won NFL co-MVP honors with Brett Favre:

201 carries, 1,103 yards, 5.5-yard average, four touchdowns.

Here are Adrian Peterson's rushing totals through the Vikings' first 10 games this season:

195 carries, 1,128 yards, 5.8 average, seven touchdowns.

Forget NFL Comeback Player of the Year. Peterson has a much bigger trophy within his powerful grasp: NFL Most Valuable Player.

"It's hard to imagine another guy having a greater impact on his team," Vikings coach Leslie Frazier said. "Especially considering where we are and what we have to do every single week to win. … He's pulling away with his domination as a runner."

Despite having his left knee surgically reconstructed in December, Peterson has accounted for 35.6 percent of his team's touches from scrimmage, 37.6 percent of its total yards and 29.1 percent of its touchdowns. Through 10 games in 1997, Sanders had accounted for 35.8 percent of the Lions' touches, 39.4 percent of its total yards and 31.2 percent of its total touchdowns.

"Watching him do what he does, he's only getting stronger as the year goes on," Vikings tight end Kyle Rudolph said of Peterson. "I think Adrian can carry us as far as Adrian wants."

Only 15 running backs — compared with 35 quarterbacks — have won The Associated Press' top individual award, which was called the "Most Outstanding Player" from 1957 to 1960 and "Most Valuable Player" beginning in 1961. Eleven of those running backs are in the Pro Football Hall of Fame and a 12th -- LaDainian Tomlinson -- will join them when he's eligible.

Peterson's 10-game start is better in terms of rushing total and average per carry than 10 of the 15 running backs who won MVP. Eight of those are Hall of Famers. One is Tomlinson.

So Peterson's start is better than Barry in 1997, Jim Taylor in 1962 (1,121, 5.7); Tomlinson in 2006 (1,037, 4.9); Emmitt Smith in 1993 (970, 5.1); Thurman Thomas in 1991 (968, 4.9); Earl Campbell in 1979 (932, 4.4); Marcus Allen in 1985 (928, 4.2); Marshall Faulk in 2000 (831, 5.2); and Paul Hornung in 1961 (518, 4.8).

And, oh yeah, Peterson's start also is better than one other pretty good player: pre-surgery Peterson, whose best 10-game start was 1,100 yards and a 4.9 average in 2008.

In other words, Peterson has done the unthinkable: He actually did get better, just as he said he would. His strength is as good as ever. His top-end speed is returning. And the road back to 100 percent actually taught him the benefits of being a more patient runner.

"There are some things that he's doing that make you scratch your head and say, 'Maybe he will be better than he was before the injury,'" Frazier said. "His hands are better, some of his cuts, his burst, he's staying more true to his reads, these are some things he hadn't done before the injury. He'd always look to hit the home run, and sometimes that would create negative plays. Now he's truer to his reads, and it's helping our offensive line to be better at what they do."

The Vikings (6-4) have twice as many victories as they had last season. But a 5-5 record and a three-game losing streak seemed like a distinct possibility midway through the fourth quarter of Sunday's game against Detroit.

The Lions had just scored a touchdown to increase their league-leading fourth-quarter point total to 111. At that point, the Vikings led 24-17 and questions abounded during a nervous few moments inside the Metrodome. Would offensive coordinator Bill Musgrave call the right plays? Would quarterback Christian Ponder show enough poise? Would the defense hold up?

No sweat. The defense watched Musgrave tell Ponder to hand Peterson the ball on six consecutive plays over two possessions. The result: 105 yards, including a 61-yard touchdown run, and a 34-17 lead. Ballgame.

"He's a joy to watch," Frazier said. "I think all of us should cherish having the chance to watch him live."

Peterson high steps into the end zone on a 61-yard touchdown run against Detroit.
JEFF WHEELER, Star Tribune

Cabbing it is Day's First Oops

Peterson's tardiness didn't go unnoticed. Nor did his 108 yards atone for two fumbles.

By MARK CRAIG/STAR TRIBUNE • November 26, 2012

CHICAGO — Adrian Peterson missed the bus Sunday.

And we're not talking about opportunities or anything like that. We're talking about a literal bus. As in the one that was supposed to transport all 53 Vikings — including the NFL's leading rusher — from the JW Marriott to Soldier Field well before a noon kickoff.

"There's something Adrian and I have to talk about regarding getting to the stadium," said Vikings coach Leslie Frazier, who clearly was not amused.

Fortunately for Peterson, Chicago is the Land of 10,000 Taxicabs. Peterson was seen flagging one of them down at about 10 a.m. and arrived at Soldier Field at 10:30 a.m., according to the NFL Network.

Frazier said he never thought about sitting Peterson for the first play or first series, which is something the Vikings typically have done when a player is late.

Peterson declined to give specifics when asked about the situation after the Vikings' 28-10 loss.

"I'm really not going to discuss that," he said. "Me and Coach actually haven't had the opportunity to talk about it. It really wasn't a big deal. Came out and played. What's important is what can we do to come back and get back on track. That's going to be our main focus."

Peterson rushed for 108 yards on 18 carries. That's a 6.0-yard average, while surpassing 100 yards for a career-record fifth consecutive game.

But it was hardly a performance worthy of celebration. Peterson was credited with losing two fumbles, giving him three this season. He admittedly was careless with the ball on the first one, while the second one bounced off his chest in a poor handoff exchange with quarterback Christian Ponder.

The Bears turned the first fumble into a 34-yard touchdown drive and a 7-3 lead in the first quarter.

"I found myself cutting to the left and got loose with the ball," Peterson said. "I guess somebody [linebacker Nick Roach] came from behind and made a good play, knocked the ball out.

"The second one was more so on me. My original landmark got kind of crashed down, so I tried to shorten my steps and the quarterback was coming one direction towards me and I'm coming towards him. And the ball hit my chest and bounced off. So that's on me."

What wasn't on Peterson was not getting a carry inside the Bears 10-yard line early in the fourth quarter. Ponder threw incomplete to receivers on third-and-2 and fourth-and-2 from the Bears 8.

"I definitely want to get the ball," Peterson said. "But [offensive coordinator Bill Musgrave] did a great job on calling plays. You think back early on in the game and it was third-down-and-4, I want to say. Great play action, we completed the ball to Kyle [Rudolph]. Came back, same play and got the score. So you live with it."

What Frazier can't live with again is Peterson missing another bus. ■

The Bears corrall Adrian Peterson in the third quarter of a 28-10 Chicago win. JERRY HOLT, Star Tribune

Left All Alone

Peterson's big day becomes a waste

By DAN WIEDERER/STAR TRIBUNE • November 12, 2012

GREEN BAY, WIS. — Pure Peterson. Truly special. You can't be serious.

Those were the thoughts circling Lambeau Field late in the first half Sunday.

Vikings star Adrian Peterson was in the south end zone hosting yet another energized party an instant after taking a handoff from Christian Ponder deep inside Vikings territory and delivering his best home run cut.

First, Peterson beat linebacker A.J. Hawk to the edge. Then he slipped an ankle tackle from Morgan Burnett. From there, he knifed between M.D. Jennings and Tramon Williams, barely felt Mike Neal's diving tackle attempt and outsprinted Casey Hayward to the end zone.

Eighty-two yards. Brilliance.

Just like that, the Vikings had a 14-10 lead over Green Bay, getting exactly the kind of big play needed to spark a road upset.

But hours later, Sunday's final score provided a 23-14 defeat, the torpedo that will likely sink the playoff ship.

Somehow, the Vikings couldn't find safety Sunday, even on a day in which Peterson registered his third career 200-yard rushing day, amassing 210 yards on 21 carries. Even on a day in which Peterson uncorked the longest run of his career — that impressive 82-yarder.

You just don't see this kind of thing often, this MVP-caliber brilliance coupled with the haphazard manner in which the Vikings have squandered it.

"It's very disappointing," Peterson said. "Especially when we run the ball like we did today. And you just look at it and say, 'It was all for nothing.'"

The unraveling again traces back to a young quarterback and a flatlining passing attack that's proven hard to revive.

Over the past six games, Peterson has rushed for 947 yards, scored six touchdowns and averaged 7.8 yards per carry. Yet over that same time, Ponder has thrown for only 871 yards with a 5.0-yards-per-attempt average.

It doesn't add up.

Said coach Leslie Frazier: "Just so disappointed that we couldn't win this game when [Adrian] had such a great day, in this environment. You want to see him celebrate. But it's so hard to celebrate after today's loss."

On Sunday, Ponder's two interceptions poisoned Peterson's punch.

The first came on the opening series of the second half, two snaps after Peterson's 48-yard run ushered the Vikings inside the Green Bay 12.

Yet on second-and-6 from the 8, Ponder rolled right, forced a throw across his body toward Michael Jenkins and was picked off in the end zone by Burnett.

"The number one rule as a quarterback," Ponder said, "is to not throw across your body, across the middle of the field."

That it was Ponder's 13th turnover in the past eight games only intensified the sting.

"We're in great position," Frazier said. "We would

have gone up 21-10 or 17-10, either way with a field goal or touchdown. The way our defense was playing, you'd love to let Jared [Allen] and those guys pin their ears back and rush at that point. But it didn't happen."

Instead, Green Bay turned that takeaway into a 47-yard field goal. Soon after, the Packers went ahead 20-14, thanks to a 22-yard James Starks touchdown run with 2:12 left in the third quarter.

And on the ensuing series, Ponder delivered his second pick, Burnett stealing a pass toward Kyle Rudolph at the Green Bay 14.

"That hurts, man," Peterson said. "You get down into the red zone, guys are playing good ball and when you turn it over, it hurts."

That's how a potentially enlivening upset bid morphs into December dejection.

Green Bay followed that second Ponder giveaway with the ultimate choke hold — an 18-play, 73-yard field goal drive that consumed the first 11 minutes of the fourth quarter.

Ponder finished with 119 passing yards — brutal on the surface but even more startling considering seven of his 12 completions and 83 of those passing yards came in the final 4 minutes. It's even more disconcerting given how Peterson was running, in theory providing the punch that should loosen things up for the passing attack.

"It's a combination of things," Frazier said. "We have to find a way to get open. We've got to do a good job in protection. And when guys are open, we've got to be able to pull the trigger and get it to them."

That's Passing 101. Yet the Vikings seem stuck at a remedial level. Even as Peterson, their premier playmaker, delivers the most splendid season of his career. ∎

Adrian Peterson takes off on an 82-yard touchdown run against Green Bay. BRIAN PETERSON, Star Tribune

Peterson Soars, But Teammates Falter

Still, star runner blames himself for loss.

By CHIP SCOGGINS/STAR TRIBUNE • December 3, 2012

GREEN BAY, WIS. — Adrian Peterson ran for the longest touchdown of his career Sunday.

He eclipsed 200 yards rushing for the third time in his career. He averaged 10 yards per carry.

He also wishes he could have done more.

Unfortunately, as great as Peterson is, he can't take the snap and throw it to himself.

Peterson registered one of the best games of his career, but the Vikings wasted it with a pathetic passing performance in a 23-14 loss to the Green Bay Packers at Lambeau Field. What a shame.

Peterson played the role of one-man wrecking crew. He tried to put the offense on his back and offset an inept passing game that offered virtually no support. He ran hard and tough and kept pounding away at a Packers defense stacked to stop him.

Peterson gave the Vikings hope with his 210 rushing yards and breathtaking 82-yard touchdown run. But Christian Ponder and his band of nonexistent receivers snuffed the life out of Peterson's efforts to record an unflattering historical achievement.

Peterson became only the third NFL running back to rush for 200 yards in a loss since 1990, joining Ricky Williams and Thomas Jones. That "feat" has happened only eight times in the modern era (since 1960).

"Oh man, it hurts," Peterson said. "Rushing yards mean nothing when you get an 'L.' It's a hard pill to swallow."

Peterson did more than that. He also shouldered blame. It's a sad commentary when he feels compelled to criticize himself for not making more big plays after putting forth maximum effort to keep his team afloat.

He lamented not being more patient on a first-down run after Harrison Smith's interception in the third quarter. Peterson picked up 6 yards on the play. He thought he should have run 94 yards for a touchdown.

And that slick 48-yard run early in the third quarter in which he avoided defenders with a perfectly executed 360 spin move? Apparently not good enough.

"Could have been faster and outrun them," Peterson said. "I feel like there's a lot of things I could have done."

That's noble of Peterson and shows his leadership and ambition to always be better. It's not his nature to engage in the blame game. But the Vikings should be embarrassed by the collection of receivers they put on the field. And Ponder's wild throws and maddening decisions undercut Peterson's brilliance to the degree that you wondered why the Vikings even call pass plays.

Peterson is a once-in-a-generation running back, and the Vikings are just squandering his talent and prime years. Peterson surpassed 8,000 yards rushing Sunday in his 85th career game, the same number of games that Emmitt Smith needed to reach that mark.

But what does Peterson have to show for it? A 45-47 record, one playoff victory and a trip to one NFC Championship Game.

If anything, the Vikings seem intent on disproving a time-honored maxim in football: A potent running game helps open things up for the passing game. Aren't those two things supposed to work hand-in-hand?

Not for the Vikings. Peterson has 100-plus rushing yards in six straight games, during which they are 2-4.

"You'd think you would be able to do whatever you want down the field with a guy rushing like that week in and week out," receiver Michael Jenkins said. "But it just hasn't materialized for whatever reason."

It's almost inconceivable that a running back can rush for 200 yards and, at the same time, a passing game can look as thoroughly incompetent as the Vikings did Sunday.

"I don't know," Peterson said when asked how that happens. "That's a good question."

Peterson turned defiant, though, when a reporter suggested that back-to-back losses to the Bears and Packers demonstrated the Vikings might not have enough talent to compete with their divisional rivals.

"Did you not see the game today?" he asked. "Did you not see how that game ended? Turnovers, penalties. That's how we lost the game. Guys fought today. We lost because we gave it to them. That was on us."

Peterson included himself in accepting blame. It was a nice gesture but entirely unnecessary. He did his part. He can't do it alone, though. ▪

Peterson grimaces on the sideline after the Vikings missed a field goal against the Packers.
CARLOS GONZALEZ, Star Tribune

Peterson Unfazed by Unreal Statistics

Star believed in himself while most doubted.

By MARK CRAIG/STAR TRIBUNE • December 7, 2012

IT'S THE MAYANS who say the world will end in 14 days. Thank goodness it's not Adrian Peterson.

Nothing that guy says sounds absurd anymore.

Better than he was before major knee surgery? Check.

Two thousand yards rushing?

Why not?

Eric Dickerson's single-season mark of 2,105 yards?

"That sounds good, too," the Vikings running back said Thursday.

Reporters chuckled. Peterson didn't.

"I'm always looking up to 2,000, 2,500 yards," Peterson said. "But I've made it real simple for myself. Go out and ball out every game. Go 100 percent with every opportunity I have and the work I've put in will show. That's all I do."

It seems ludicrous now to think that Peterson's mere presence in uniform on opening day was hailed as a grand accomplishment just three months ago.

Peterson told us there would be more to the story. Much more. But who truly believed that a 27-year-old four-time All-Pro would run with just as much power, more speed and much more patience than he did before tearing the anterior cruciate and medial collateral ligaments in his left knee last Christmas Eve?

"Through the midst of it, you only have to have one believer," Peterson said. "I definitely believed."

He hasn't walked on water. But he has run for 1,446 yards and a 6.2-yard average. Right now, the silver rushing medal belongs to Seattle's Marshawn Lynch, who trails by 308 yards and 1.6 yards per carry.

Heck, 22 entire teams trail Peterson in rushing yards. And quarterback Christian Ponder has 76 fewer yards passing (871) than Peterson has rushing (947) during his current franchise-record streak of six consecutive 100-yard games.

When it comes to power, Peterson still has that. In yards after first contact, he ranks No. 1 in the league with a 3.2-yard average.

When it comes to speed, he might not be the fastest player in the league, but he does have a league-high 17 rushes of 20 yards or more, including runs of 48, 61, 64, 74 and a career-best 82-yarder for a touchdown in last week's loss at Green Bay.

"Do I feel faster?" Peterson said. "Not necessarily. I don't know. If I am, I really can't tell that big a difference."

Fast is faster than the nearest defender in the open field. And Peterson isn't being caught like he was early in the season.

With the way he has played the past six games, Peterson said he doesn't have to think about the magical number 2,000.

"I'm making it simple for myself," Peterson said. "Just continue to play the way I've been playing and it will come naturally."

Peterson is on pace for 1,928 yards. That would be the eighth-best rushing performance in league history and 168 yards better than his franchise record set in 2008.

He's averaging 120.5 yards per game. If he bumps that average to 138.5 over the final four games, he would become the seventh player to reach 2,000 yards, moving ahead of Earl Campbell (1,934).

If he averages 140.8, he would move into fourth place ahead of O.J. Simpson (2,003), Chris Johnson (2,006) and Terrell Davis (2,008). And if he averages 165 yards, he would set the record, surpassing Barry Sanders (2,053), Jamal Lewis (2,066) and Dickerson, whose mark was set in 1984, a year before Peterson was born.

How far-fetched is that? Well, his average the past six games is 157.8. And he's coming off a 210-yard game. And, well, he's Adrian Peterson, NFL Nostradamus.

Peterson also doesn't appear hung up on statistics.

"I want to win a couple championships," he said when asked what his goals are. "I feel like it can happen here. We have the talent to make it happen. ... However long it takes, I'm going to ride it till the wheels fall off."

The left wheel did come off last Christmas Eve. But Peterson just put it back on and kept going. ■

CARLOS GONZALEZ, Star Tribune

'Bread-and-Butter' Play Sets Stage

A 51-yard run gives Peterson a boost in his quest for the rushing title.

By MARK CRAIG/STAR TRIBUNE • December 10, 2012

THE VIKINGS opened Sunday's game against the Bears with a play they call "34 Doctor."

It's an ordinary play, but in the hands of an extraordinary running back such as Adrian Peterson it can and did become a 51-yard tone-setter that the Vikings rode to a 21-14 victory at Mall of America Field.

"'Doctor' is just smash-mouth football at its best," right guard Brandon Fusco said. "It's a bread-and-butter play for us."

The Vikings had first-and-10 from their 20 on the game's first play from scrimmage. The Bears had six players on the line of scrimmage and nine in the box. The Vikings countered with three tight ends to block the edge and a plan for right tackle Phil Loadholt to block down and help Fusco double-team nose tackle Matt Toeaina.

"All we have to do is give Adrian a little crease," Loadholt said. "He's always telling us, 'Just give me that little crease.'"

When Loadholt blocked down on Toeaina, he was able to wall off linebacker Lance Briggs inside as well. That became a key block when tight end John Carlson was able to hook block linebacker Geno Hayes, creating a lane for Peterson to run through. Rookie tight end Rhett Ellison took care of middle linebacker Nick Roach, who was starting in place of the injured Brian Urlacher.

"I didn't know for sure if [Hayes] was going to get hooked, but on this particular play he did," Peterson said. "I'm reading it out. My eyes go from [the end] to the tackle."

It was outstanding blocking that left Peterson one on one with safety Chris Conte. Peterson stiff-armed Conte to the ground and took off before finally being run out of bounds by Briggs and cornerback Charles Tillman.

"That's the definition of starting fast," quarterback Christian Ponder said. "The guy is unbelievable."

Peterson went on to set a franchise record for most yards in the first quarter. He had 104, breaking his own mark of 96 set Nov. 4 at Seattle.

The Vikings ran 15 first-quarter plays, and Peterson carried the ball on 12 of them. He also had both touchdowns on a pair of 1-yard runs as the Vikings led 14-0.

That's not easy. Not when every defense is designed specifically to stop Peterson.

"It's all willpower," Peterson said. "They pretty much know we're going to run the ball."

Peterson finished with 154 yards on a career-high 31 carries. He extended his franchise record for most consecutive 100-yard games to seven. In those seven games, he has run for 1,101 yards, an average of 157.3 per game.

Peterson has a league-high 1,600 yards with three games left. He needs to average 133.3 yards to reach 2,000 and 168.7 to break Eric Dickerson's NFL mark of 2,105 yards.

"I think about [2,000 yards], but I don't try to think about it too much," Peterson said. "I feel like it will happen. Like I said, it's obvious we're going to continue to run the ball." ■

Adrian Peterson celebrates his first touchdown against the Bears. BRIAN PETERSON, Star Tribune

Rompin', Stompin'

Everyone's getting a rush watching Peterson's pursuit.

By JIM SOUHAN/STAR TRIBUNE • December 17, 2012

ST. LOUIS — Adrian Peterson is redefining the phrase "runner's high." It's those who watch him run who become lightheaded.

Peterson is making oxygen debt a communal experience. When he runs, people on couches across Minnesota gasp for breath.

Sunday, Peterson found another way to share endorphins, this time rushing for 212 yards and a touchdown to beat a St.Louis Rams team dedicated to stopping him, leading the Vikings to a 36-22 victory at the Edward Jones Dome.

It didn't matter that the Rams lined up with five defensive linemen to start the game. Or that his first seven carries netted zero yards. Or that handing the ball to Peterson is as predictable a strategy as running attack ads during an election.

With his latest improbable outburst, Peterson reached a personal-best 1,812 yards for the season, leaving him 293 shy of Eric Dickerson's NFL record of 2,105 with two games remaining. Considering he's averaged 164 yards a game for the past eight weeks, Peterson could downshift into history.

"He's going to get the record," rookie left tackle Matt Kalil said. "But what I know is that what he really cares about is winning games."

The two pursuits aren't mutually exclusive on a Vikings team that again averaged more yards when handing the ball to Peterson (8.2) than when Christian Ponder attempted a pass (5.5).

St. Louis hadn't allowed a back to rush for more than 65 yards in its previous four games. Peterson beat that total with his second-quarter 82-yard touchdown run.

Center John Sullivan asked for Peterson's total, then nodded. "We're getting close," he said. "And we got the win, which was the most important part.

"We knew coming in that St. Louis was a really, really good defense. They're chippy. That have that mentality that the Titans used to have. They're going to trash talk, they're going to get in some extra shots after the whistle. There's some unpredictability there, so we were going to have some plays for zero and minus-1. We say feast or famine. So we found that big run, and that was the feast."

After five of his first seven carries went for losses, Peterson became a glutton. His eighth carry went for 8 yards. His ninth went for 82. His last 17 carries of the day went for 212.

On his 82-yarder, the Rams dropped back to cover the pass and fullback Jerome Felton obliterated Wayzata's own James Laurinaitis, the Rams' standout linebacker.

"My fullback, Felton, is playing outstanding," Peterson said. "That first touchdown, that was a brutal block he laid on 55."

Peterson's most important run didn't take him to the end zone, but it kept the Vikings in the playoff race. The Rams had closed to 33-22 midway through the fourth quarter. The Vikings took over at their 20.

Peterson took a handoff left and found nothing but blue jerseys. He reversed field, shrugged off a tackle in the backfield and burst through the right side for 52 yards. It was his last carry of the game. It led to a field goal and locker room filled with hope.

"That play was insane," Sullivan said. "Just insane. Our running game is in a special place right now."

Peterson said he could have "run for 300" yards, and admitted he has eyed Dickerson's record. He called the former Ram, "Such a great back, and a guy I looked up to, and who inspired me to work toward greatness. To surpass him would definitely be great. It's been there since, what, '84? I was born a year later, and that's when I started my journey to get here."

A half-hour after the game, St. Louis finally stopped Peterson. First, a boy asking for an autograph interrupted his trek to the team bus, then a host of others came forward for signatures or handshakes, and soon Peterson found himself amid 15 military people in fatigues, posing for photos.

You've got to swarm him to slow him down and, as the Rams learned, sometimes even that doesn't work. "Even if you know what's coming, you can't stop it," Kalil said. "At this point, nobody's going to stop him."

Adrian Peterson throws one of his cleats to a fan after the win in St. Louis. CARLOS GONZALEZ, Star Tribune

Can Peterson Beat Manning for MVP?

Rarely has the league's most valuable player not led his team to the playoffs.

By MARK CRAIG/STAR TRIBUNE • December 19, 2012

CAN RUNNING BACK Adrian Peterson win the NFL Most Valuable Player award if the Vikings don't make the playoffs?

Yes, but he'd be 96.5 percent better off if he concluded this year's magic act by reaching into his top hat and pulling Christian Ponder into the playoffs with a 10-6 record.

There have been 57 winners in the 55 years that the Associated Press has recognized an MVP (1961-present) or a Most Outstanding Player (1957-1960). Only two of them — 3.5 percent — were on teams that didn't make it to the postseason.

In 1973, O.J. Simpson's Buffalo Bills went 9-5 the year he became the first player to rush for 2,000 yards (2,003). At the time, there was only one wild card per conference. Had there been two, as there has since 1978, the Bills would have made the playoffs.

Johnny Unitas' Baltimore Colts (11-1-2) tied the Los Angeles Rams atop the Western Conference's Coastal Division in 1967. The Colts missed the playoffs because the Rams had a 24-point net difference in head-to-head games.

The Vikings are 8-6 and can make the playoffs as a wild card only. Even that would make Peterson a rare winner of the award.

Since wild cards were introduced with the AFL-NFL merger in 1970, only six of 44 MVPs have come from a wild-card team. The last to do so was Peyton Manning,

whose third of four MVPs came during the Colts' 12-4 season in 2008.

Four running backs have won MVP while playing for a wild-card team. Barry Sanders (1997) and Walter Payton (1977) did it on 9-7 teams. That's more than twice the average number of losses for a team that has the MVP (three).

Impatience is a modern societal flaw. So it's no wonder people can't wait two more games before demanding to know if Peterson is the MVP winner.

As someone who has a vote for the award, the answer from this vantage point goes something like this: "Easy, pal. The season isn't over."

Peterson is in good position to win. But so is two-time winner Tom Brady, four-time winner Manning and reigning MVP Aaron Rodgers.

Peterson has 1,812 yards and a 6.3-yard average against stacked defenses that have absolutely no fear of Ponder hurting them with the deep pass. Even more amazing is the fact that Peterson has averaged 171 yards per game and has topped 200 twice while leading the Vikings to a 3-2 record without Percy Harvin.

Manning, of course, has outdone himself while playing for the hottest team in the league, the 11-3 Broncos. Manning won MVPs in Indianapolis with replaceable parts at receiver, running back and offensive line. Who knew he could change entire franchises and never miss a beat?

Like Manning, Rodgers and Brady have carried their teams to division titles already. Meanwhile, Peterson's team isn't nearly as good, yet it's still playing meaningful games in late December.

But is that enough? The MVP is an individual award, but the individual's performance has to carry his team to extraordinary — not good — heights. That's why 37 quarterbacks with a combined record of 470-102-4 (.819) have been selected.

There are exceptions, of course. If the Vikings don't make the playoffs, Peterson's case would be similar to Simpson's in 1973 if Peterson were to break Eric Dickerson's single-season rushing record of 2,105.

Before Simpson's 1973 season, Jim Brown's mark of 1,863 yards was the rushing standard. Simpson came along and averaged 143.1 yards per game, 10 more than Brown.

Peterson is averaging 129.4 and needs 294 to break Dickerson's mark. If Peterson gets the mark and doesn't win MVP, he'll have some Hall of Fame company. The year Dickerson set the record, 1984, he led the Rams to a wild-card berth but was trumped for MVP by Dan Marino, who won a division title while setting a single-season passing mark (5,089 yards) that stood until last year.

There are so many variables to consider over the next two weeks. But there is one scenario that's a no-brainer to this brain: If Peterson breaks the record and leads the throwback Vikings to a playoff berth in this pass-crazed league, well, he's got my vote. ■

Peterson finishes an 82-yard touchdown run against the Rams. CARLOS GONZALEZ, Star Tribune

Runaway Winner

Peterson, the first two-time recipient of the Star Tribune award that started in 1998.

By DAN WIEDERER/STAR TRIBUNE • December 23, 2012

ADRIAN PETERSON is given a piece of paper.

On it, written in black Sharpie, is a number: 18,355.

Peterson easily recognizes it.

"Oh yeah," he says, growing almost giddy. "Emmitt Smith."

Those 18,355 yards measure Smith's NFL career rushing record, a landmark near the top of Peterson's "Become The Greatest Of All Time" checklist.

He stares at the total.

"Reachable," he asserts. "It can happen."

With that number, Peterson is also given a date: Sunday, Sept. 29, 2019. This is foreign to the Vikings star, prompting a quizzical look.

It's explained that if he stays on his remarkable career pace of 98.448275 rushing yards per game and doesn't miss a single contest in the next six-plus seasons, he will be in position to break Smith's record in Week 4 of 2019.

Peterson looks up with a grin, then shrugs. He's appreciative of the math but far from accepting of it.

He looks back down at the number, then taps the date. "Sooner than that," he says. "For real. Sooner."

Are you going to be the one to tell Adrian Peterson he's being overly ambitious? That his competitive drive is skewing reality? Or after witnessing him make good on so many promises this year, will you simply nod and trust that his word is as firm as his python-grip handshake?

"I'm not sure how fast I can get there," Peterson says. "I have to crunch some numbers myself. But I'll do some research and get back to you with my date."

It's little wonder Peterson was the runaway choice as the Star Tribune's 2012 Sportsperson of the Year. He could have won the award based on contagious optimism alone.

After all, on Jan. 1 Peterson woke up in an Alabama hospital bed and pledged — as so many do when the calendar flips — to attack the new year with so much purpose and so little fear.

Yet unlike most of the world, he found rare mental reserves to sustain his drive.

When everyone else saw a career-threatening ACL injury, Peterson saw a challenge to come back stronger, quicker and more determined.

He now has sprinted to the front of the NFL's Most Valuable Player race.

And when everyone else saw a rebuilding Vikings team that would be fortunate to win six games, Peterson saw little time to waste and strived to propel a playoff push.

Now, with two games left, the 8-6 Vikings find themselves gripping the NFC's final wild-card spot — with Peterson on an unprecedented tear, totaling 1,313 yards and nine touchdowns in the past eight games alone.

So why wouldn't Emmitt Smith's record seem attainable?

Says Vikings coach Leslie Frazier: "Obviously, 2019 is a long way off. But I know Adrian and the way he thinks. He can't fathom that it will take him that long. Not him. So, hey ..."

BRIAN PETERSON, Star Tribune

That's the thing about Peterson. He has this persuasive power and a unique way of warping time.

Somehow, at the end of this extraordinary year, he can talk about potential 2019 achievements as if they were just around the corner while in the same conversation make Dec. 24, 2011, seem so far, far, far in the past.

Adrian Peterson has been given a full tank of positive energy.
It never depletes either.

Last Christmas Eve, an ill-timed hit by Washington's DeJon Gomes left Peterson with torn anterior cruciate and medial collateral ligaments in his left knee.

In the weeks that followed, all logical Peterson discussions carried a glum theme: whether one of the all-time greats had his brilliance stolen from him in his prime.

Now, one day from the anniversary of that setback, the entire Peterson conversation centers on whether he can complete the greatest rushing season in history, needing 294 yards to break Eric Dickerson's single-season record of 2,105 yards.

Says left tackle Matt Kalil: "The way he's going? He'll blow by that. Easily."

Peterson learned long ago that even seemingly unfathomable goals can be attained with precise mind calibration. Crank the willpower and enthusiasm dials up, turn the hesitance down.

It's part of what Frazier calls Peterson's "name it and claim it" achievement system.

"It all starts with faith in God and believing," Peterson says. "And having that confidence that no matter what happens throughout your life, you can bounce back and refocus and continue to have faith that you can accomplish all things."

Peterson realizes it sounds odd. But he's certain he fortified this mindset as a kid in Texas, just 7 years old when he saw his older brother, Brian, be hit by a drunken driver while riding his bike.

Within a week, Brian died. At age 8.

Peterson was crushed.

Yet even as a 7-year-old, he darted around self-pity and ran right over his grief. Peterson struggled to accept Brian's death but knew he couldn't wallow when his mother's anguish required soothing.

"I had to be so strong during that time," he says. "I had to be positive and constantly reassure my mom everything was going to be OK. Instead of beating myself up and crying the whole year 'round over my brother's death, I told myself to use it as motivation, use it to be positive."

Then in seventh grade, when his father, Nelson, went to prison on a felony conviction of laundering drug money, Adrian took a similar approach.

"I said, 'Ya know what? I'm going to make my dad happy,'" Peterson says. "He made a mistake, and his own choices put him in that situation. But I went about looking at it in a different way, like there was a new motivation for me.

"I've been doing that my whole life."

Adrian Peterson has been given unbridled tenacity.
Maybe it's part stubbornness, too — with a unique combination of anger and persistence mixed in. Whatever it is, Peterson hates accepting defeat.

It's why, after rushing for 210 yards in a 23-14 loss at Green Bay in Week 13, he stood in front of his locker still insisting he should have done more, asserting that a 6-yard third-quarter run should have easily gone for 94 and lamenting that his 48-yard burst a few possessions earlier hadn't reached the end zone — which, of course, would have rescued Christian Ponder from subsequently throwing an upset-killing interception in the end zone.

"When things go wrong," Peterson says, "I choose to focus on the things I could be doing better."

To be clear, Peterson's positivity isn't unshakable. Frazier absorbed the brunt of the running back's ire on the first night of training camp when the Vikings made the medically-advised-but-still-tough-to-deliver decision that Peterson would open camp on the physically-unable-to-perform list.

It was a move that would confine Peterson to doing strength and conditioning and additional rehabilitation work on the side.

Like a cartoon character, the smoke blew from Peterson's ears with a train-whistle shriek.

Recalls Frazier: "Ohhh. He was livid. [It was] 'You're holding me back! Why are you doing this to me?'"

"I was hot," Peterson confesses. "Furious. I can't deny

that. It was a lose-lose for me. I no longer had control. It's not like I was going to refuse going on PUP. But I was angry because I felt I was ready. I knew I was ready."

Still, rather than act out or pout, Peterson lay down that night and figured out a way to win. He was having no luck quelling his urge to be back in practice with the guys.

"So I changed my view of the situation," Peterson says. "It was like, if I'm going to be working out over here on the side, I'll work way harder than those guys are practicing."

Vikings athletic trainer Eric Sugarman and strength coach Tom Kanavy knew they would have a rodeo bull to tame. But who doesn't like a challenge to break up the monotony of training camp? So with hopes of channeling Peterson's intensity in the right direction, Sugarman and Kanavy plotted numerous ways to exhaust the running back.

Instead, it was Peterson exhausting every test, every drill, every apparatus they found for him.

Kanavy says he went through "the whole toy box of extra stuff." Quick foot ladders, speed ladders, kettle bells, battle ropes.

"We got to the point where we started taking the weights on the field," Kanavy says, "because Adrian had already blown through the resistant running and the parachute running and the pushing sleds, pulling sleds.

"If it had gone on any longer, I was going to have to start throwing rocks at him or something. Because we'd used everything else we had."

The Vikings kept waiting for the moment where Peterson would return from the previous day's grueling workout and acknowledge significant fatigue or soreness or burnout.

It never came.

Says Sugarman: "Sometimes the most fun part of this job is trying to challenge these guys, to try to break them. Adrian's not breakable."

Adrian Peterson has been given a golden opportunity this season. And the proper perspective to soak it all in.
On Aug. 12, a few days before training camp broke, Peterson was let out of the chute for his first practice. And even without testing himself in preseason action, he was, as he had always promised he would be, in the starting lineup Sept. 9 for the opener against Jacksonville.

As the Vikings offensive starters were announced, Peterson stood in the tunnel at Mall of America Field and flashed back to the hospital and the surgery and the moments he began envisioning his return.

"It had always seemed so far away," he says.

Now, it had arrived.

"Literally being at the end of that tunnel," Peterson says, "seeing the lights, seeing the fans, hearing it get louder and seeing my guys out there waiting for me to run through, it was like redemption."

Peterson ran for 84 yards and two touchdowns that day, breaking off a 20-yarder in overtime to spark the game-winning drive.

In truth, that could have been a triumphant exclamation point, Peterson's recovery completed faster than anyone imagined.

A solid 1,000-yard season would have been universally applauded. But a return wasn't all Peterson promised. He had also vowed to be better than before.

So he kept pushing, kept getting stronger, and before anyone knew it, he had begun a torrid stretch in which he smashed a team record with eight consecutive 100-yard rushing games — and still counting. During the surge, he has averaged 7.5 yards per carry and 164 yards per game, also tying an NFL single-season record with seven runs of longer than 50 yards.

Adrian Peterson has been given respect.
Teammates and coaches have come to appreciate Peterson's dominance through different vantage points. Defensive end Jared Allen, for example, has spent five seasons enjoying the show.

"It's like, 'When is he going to break the next one? Oh, there he goes,'" Allen says. "I always tell him he needs to rest up. Because if I was the offensive coordinator, he'd carry the ball 75 times a game. I mean, look what he's doing. It's amazing. I just want to see it. I'm a fan."

Kalil? He's been a part of Peterson's mastery for all of 14 games and could only laugh in the locker room last Sunday after Peterson demoralized the Rams with 212 rushing yards.

"It's kind of getting old," Kalil says, mostly joking. "He's so good ... I'm following him downfield. It's like front row seats for the best movie ever."

And then there's Frazier, whose impressive ability to stabilize and focus a team would seem so much less significant if he didn't have the playmaker in the 28 jersey to lean on.

Frazier calls Peterson "a great player who guys gravitate to and love to play with."

"The way our team has stuck together throughout the year, even during bumps in the road, is a direct reflection of Adrian's approach," Frazier says. "The football part is amazing. We're all in awe of his accomplishments. But his humility and his style of leadership resonates."

Frazier pauses, searching for the most complete way to express his appreciation.

"It's rare that a guy of this magnitude is as gracious as Adrian," he says. "Over time, I've been around some very good players. And they make it clear in no uncertain terms that it's about them. All about them. Adrian is not like that."

So now come those three letters: MVP, a title Peterson has every right to claim for the first time this season.

Ask him about it and he insists he has higher goals: reaching the playoffs and making a run at the Super Bowl.

Sure, that sentiment is sincere. But don't think for a second it means Peterson doesn't care at all about being named MVP. Remember, he doesn't respond well to not winning.

You may not recall 2004, when after rushing for 1,925 yards and 15 touchdowns as a freshman at Oklahoma, Peterson finished as runner-up to Southern California's Matt Leinart for the Heisman Trophy. But Peterson does.

"I feel like I got robbed," he says, shaking his head as if the announcement had just come. "Without question. I was robbed. And it still bothers me."

Then, as usual, he shrugs.

"But I guess I can look at it like this. At least Matt Leinart has something he can look back on and say, 'Bam! I won a Heisman Trophy.'"

Perhaps Peterson soon will have to convince himself to feel similarly pleased for Peyton Manning, Aaron Rodgers or Tom Brady. So be it.

"In my mind," he says, "whether I get the MVP or not, I'm a winner. Just look at my story. I don't really feel like I have to say much." ■

CARLOS GONZALEZ, Star Tribune

Once More, with Meaning

Peterson's indescribable, but why not give it a shot?

By MARK CRAIG/STAR TRIBUNE • December 30, 2012

YEARS AGO, Browns Hall of Famer Jim Brown was sitting in a small interview room in Berea, Ohio, trying to forearm shiver some sense into a young reporter too caught up in comparing great running backs.

"Why," said the man generally considered the greatest running back of all-time, "would you want to take away from one great running style by trying to compare it to another great running style?"

Because, um, that's kind of what we non-runners without great styles like to do between opening kickoffs.

"You can't make comparisons," Brown said. "A great running style is like a fingerprint or a voice on the phone that you know without having to look at the person's face. You should recognize it and enjoy the greatness without judging it against greatness that came before it or the greatness that will come later on."

Great running styles often can be summed up in one word. Brown was overpowering, like a man among children. Barry Sanders was nimble, like a ballerina in a bowling ball's body. Gale Sayers slashed and O.J. Simpson dashed. Earl Campbell was unbridled while Eric Dickerson was smooth.

The position faded as the NFL shifted to a passing league long ago. But something unusual has happened this season. At a point when all of us thought it was impossible for a running back to lead a rebuilding, one-dimensional throwback team to the brink of the playoffs, along came Adrian Peterson, a guy whose do-it-all style has proven difficult to sum up in one word.

"I'd say 'powerful,'" said quarterback Christian Ponder. "But it's a combination of power and agility. So I don't know."

"You want my one word?" asked right guard Brandon Fusco. "How about, `Wow?'"

"`Violent,'" said fullback Jerome Felton. "Definitely 'violent.' "

RECORD CHASE

WITH 1,898 YARDS, Peterson stands one monster game from making this a season that would be remembered as the greatest by a running back in NFL history.

With a victory and 208 yards rushing in Sunday's game against the Packers at Mall of America Field, Peterson would break Dickerson's single-season rushing record of 2,105 yards, most likely clinch league's MVP and, oh yeah, lift the Vikings to a 10-6 record and the NFC's sixth playoff seed.

"I'd be satisfied with both," Peterson said with a

smile. "I feel like I have a good chance. I believe it. And in order to accomplish it, you got to believe it."

Since tearing the anterior cruciate and medial collateral ligaments in his left knee on Christmas Eve a year ago, Peterson has proven the only thing that matters is what he believes is possible.

"There's a reason none of us believed him when he said he would come back better than ever, which he has," said Vikings personnel consultant Paul Wiggin. "The reason is no one could fathom that happening. To anyone. Ever."

Coach Leslie Frazier admits he wasn't sure what to expect.

"Adrian plants his feet and cuts harder than anyone I've ever seen," Frazier said. "Barry [Sanders] was a guy who was always cutting and darting, too. But not as violently. Barry was nimble. Adrian sticks that foot in the ground hard. It made me hold my breath until I saw him do it enough times."

Early in the rehabilitation process, Frazier approached Peterson about the possibility of having to change his running style. The conversation didn't last long.

Peterson said he doesn't remember Frazier bringing it up. Frazier remembers Peterson saying four words.

"He said, 'I don't think so,'" Frazier said. "And then what does he do? He comes back with the very same running style and he's [102] yards from 2,000."

WORD GAMES

MEANWHILE, teammates are still searching for that one word.

"`Explosive,'" says center John Sullivan. "But he's so well-rounded. He can play every style. I need more than one word."

Sorry. We're tight on space. Next.

"Is 'downhill' one word?" asked left guard Charlie Johnson. "If not, give me 'angry.' He runs like he's mad. Like he's going to beat someone up."

Rookie left tackle Matt Kalil said, 'Nonstop,' but then became distracted when told that Texans running back Arian Foster bought his offensive linemen Segways.

"Adrian will take care of us," Kalil said. "Especially if he gets that record. I might get a car."

Packers coach Mike McCarthy wasted no time picking a word to describe Peterson's style. It was fitting for the man who has rushed for 1,243 yards and eight touchdowns on 223 carries (5.6 yards per attempt) in 11 games against the Packers.

"Attacking," McCarthy said. "There's not enough recognition about his vision. His ability to see the second man. In my opinion, the great ones don't only worry about the first guy. The way he attacks the defense, he's extremely unique in that way."

Peterson is four weeks removed from blasting the Packers for 210 yards on just 21 carries. He's also running where he set the NFL single-game rushing record of 296 yards as a rookie.

But the Packers come into the game with a determination not to be embarrassed again. They also come in with Clay Matthews, who was injured and missed the first meeting.

"Clay Matthews is our best player on our defense and he's an impact player," McCarthy said. "Anytime he's on the field, we're a better football team."

Meanwhile, Vikings right tackle Phil Loadholt gives up on the pursuit of a fancy one-word answer and says, "It's simple, but 'Hard.'" Running backs coach James Saxon says, "Easy. 'Fantastic.' " But former Vikings running back Chuck Foreman negotiates an extra word.

"I'll say, 'Aggressively aggressive,' " he said. "When a guy is that committed and works that hard, never bet against him. When the Lord made Adrian, he threw away that mold for sure."

A LITTLE SWEETNESS

SORRY, JIM, but the urge to compare is sometimes too great.

Frazier compares Peterson to Walter Payton, whom

he played with in Chicago.

" 'Competitor' is the word I'd use for Walter," Frazier said. "A guy trying to tackle him, Walter wanted to run over him. A guy trying to outrun Walter? He wanted to outrun him. He always in his mind that, 'I'm going to be the best.' "

And Peterson?

" 'Focused' is how I'd describe Adrian," Frazier said. "Or, actually, 'Determined,' might be the better word. Very determined. He's a lot like Walter."

Wiggin played for the Browns throughout Brown's entire nine-year career (1957-65) in Cleveland.

"The word I'd use for Jim is, 'War,' " Wiggin said. "One of the greatest runs Jim Brown ever had went for 2 yards. He beat back about five guys and took it into the end zone for a touchdown."

And Peterson?

"I'd say, 'Obsessed,' " Wiggin said. "He and Jim are so much alike. So many times, Adrian will do something and I'll say to myself, 'Jim Brown.'

"If you remember that run in Cleveland [in 2009], when Adrian used his forearm to club that defender out of bounds. That was so Jim Brown."

OK, Jim. We're done comparing. We have only one person left to weigh in.

One word, Adrian. Go.

"Vicious," he said to a scrum of reporters who then set the North American land speed record for tweeting a player's answer to a question. "I guess you can say that."

Yes, Adrian, you definitely can say that. ■

Peterson enters the season finale 208 yards away from the single-season rushing record. BRIAN PETERSON, Star Tribune

With Peterson Hemmed in, Offense Excels Outside the Box

His streak of 100-yard games ended, Christian Ponder found other outlets, and backup.

By MARK CRAIG/STAR TRIBUNE • December 24, 2012

HOUSTON — This is how the Vikings offense should look when teams consistently commit eight and nine defenders to stopping Adrian Peterson.

That's why the soon-to-be five-time All-Pro running back was still smiling on a day when he failed to gain 100 yards for the first time in nine weeks. That's also why he called the 9-6 Vikings a playoff-worthy team on a day when their best player matched his worst rushing average of the season.

"It felt good to see other guys get involved," Peterson said after the Vikings' 23-6 victory over the Texans at Reliant Stadium. "It felt good for us to continue moving the ball down the field and get some points."

The Vikings' two biggest victories of the season came against the 49ers in Week 3 and the Texans on Sunday. Ironically, Peterson's rushing numbers were the same in both games: 25 carries for 86 yards, no touchdowns and a season-low 3.4 average.

With 1,898 yards this season, Peterson heads into Sunday's season finale against the visiting Packers needing 102 yards to become the seventh NFL player to rush for 2,000 yards and 208 to break Eric Dickerson's single-season mark of 2,105.

Oh, and by the way, Peterson had 210 yards on 21 carries at Green Bay 22 days ago.

"Of course, I care about [the record]," Peterson said. "But I'm not going to let it overwhelm me. I'll get some rest and be ready to get the 'W' and break that record."

The Texans came into Sunday's game ranked fifth against the run with a 93.2-yard average. They had nine players in the box on the Vikings' first play from scrimmage.

Peterson went 20 yards anyway. He also sprinkled in additional runs of 20 and 21 yards, extending his NFL-best runs of 20 yards to 23.

But Peterson also was stopped for no gain or losses on 14 of his 25 carries. Those 14 carries, all of which came against at least eight defenders in the box or a cornerback blitzing off the edge, went for minus-14 yards total, while 22 of his 25 carries went for only 25 yards.

"Obviously, we're happy to hold him under 100 yards," said Texans defensive end J.J. Watt. "But we're not happy with the results of the overall game."

With Peterson drawing so much attention, the Vikings

had perfect balance. They rushed for 174 yards on 42 carries (4.1) while Christian Ponder passed for 174 yards. Ponder also ran seven times for 48 yards.

"Christian's a young guy who is playing with more passion and showing more desire, having more confidence in what he can do," Peterson said. "He's taking chances. Sometimes, you're like, 'Ahhh.' But that's everybody. It just gets pointed out more at the quarterback position. But he's been outstanding these past couple weeks."

Peterson's final carry of the game came with 6 minutes, 46 seconds left. Rather than risk further aggravating Peterson's abdomen injury, the Vikings turned to backup Toby Gerhart, who matched a season high for carries (eight) while rushing for 31 yards and his first touchdown of the season.

"I was a little sore, but nothing too serious," Peterson said of his abdomen. "It's been bothering me the past couple of weeks. I feel we made the best decision. Toby did a good job of sticking the dagger in them. So mission completed." ▪

Peterson rushed for 86 yards against Houston. CARLOS GONZALEZ, Star Tribune

Encore! Encore!

Peterson fell a few yards short of history but carried team to a more important milestone.

By DAN WIEDERER/STAR TRIBUNE • December 31, 2012

AS A WONDERFUL mix of pride and euphoria swirled through the Vikings locker room Sunday evening, a quest for explanations began..

In so many ways, the scene made so little sense. The NFL's most surprising team of 2012 had won the right to keep playing into 2013, upsetting rival Green Bay 37-34 on a last-second 29-yard field goal by Blair Walsh.

That provided the climax to a wildly entertaining, often confusing and incredibly stressful day in which the Vikings never trailed but never felt completely safe either.

Walsh's kick triggered fireworks, then provided an even more notable locker room eruption at Mall of America Field.

Somehow, these Vikings are one of 12 teams left with a chance to win the Super Bowl.

"How about those Vikings, huh?" head coach Leslie Frazier said with a double fist pump.

Sunday's triumph — more improbable in its form than in its result — provided the Vikings a 10th win and created a playoff rematch with the Packers next Saturday night at Lambeau Field.

So it was worth asking: How in the world did all this happen?

"That's a great question," 14th-year veteran Antoine Winfield said. "I don't know."

Even the players who hustled and fought to collect each of the 10 victories and who have preached for months about the values of belief and unity confess that this extraordinary run is now stretching even their imaginations.

Winfield did what many pro athletes do, issuing a reminder that the Vikings have quieted their doubters.

"I'm sure none of you had us picked to get into the playoffs," he said.

Yeah, but Antoine, in August how much of a chance did you give this team to win 10 times and reach the playoffs?

"Small percentage," he confessed. "But it happened."

Jared Allen searched for his own ways to explain the turnaround — from 3-13 last season to 10-6 now, from the NFC North cellar to an express ramp that has them gaining momentum and confidence for the playoffs. Yet as Allen tried to convey his pride in this team's work ethic and focus, he eventually opted for an idiom borrowed from fellow defensive lineman Fred Evans.

"Ain't no couches in the ocean, playa," Allen said with a laugh. "So you better sink or swim."

Owner Zygi Wilf has made a habit this season of giving his tie away after victories to that day's hero. But Wilf would have needed a U-Haul to bring enough neckwear to reward all those worthy Sunday.

Walsh, for one, not only kicked the game-winner but opened the scoring with a 54-yard field goal, his 10th straight make from 50 yards or beyond.

And how would any recap be complete without glowing exaltation of Adrian Peterson, whose chase of Eric

Adrian Peterson celebrates the win over Green Bay with teammate Jamarca Sanford.
ELIZABETH FLORES, Star Tribune

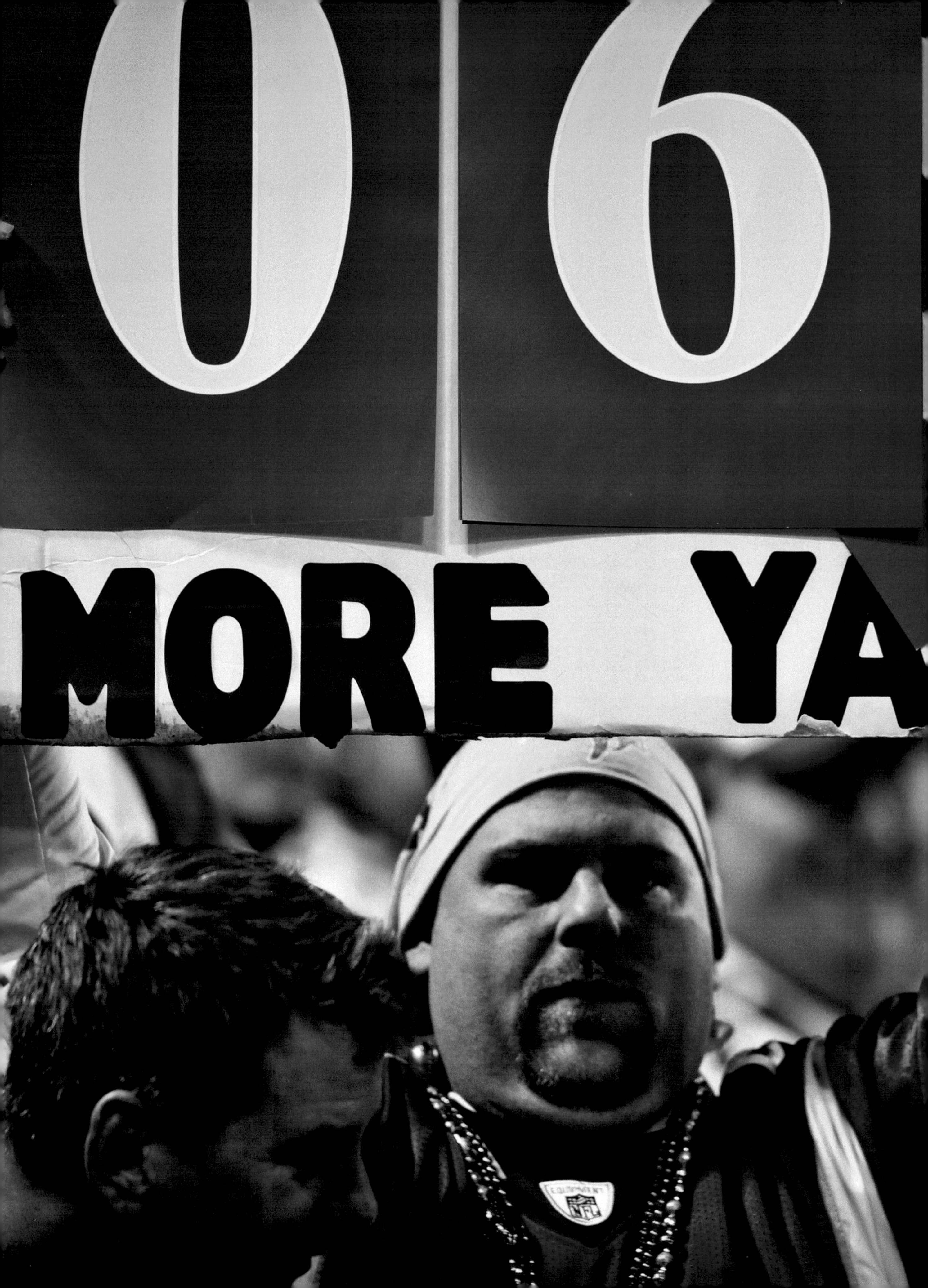
0 6
MORE YA
NFL

Dickerson's single-season rushing record came up 8 yards short. But did that really matter after Peterson supplied 199 rushing yards, including 26 on his final carry? He also scored twice — on a 7-yard run and a 2-yard catch.

And a single-season rushing total of 2,097 yards plus the magnetic optimism that Peterson has used to drive this team certainly merited the "M-V-P" chants that bounced around the Metrodome.

The running back heard those. "I was really just taking in all the love they were showing me," Peterson said.

Sunday's love also went toward Jarius Wright, who not only caught an 8-yard TD in the second quarter but delivered the Vikings' longest catch this season — a 65-yarder in the fourth quarter during a key tiebreaking touchdown drive.

Sunday's love also belonged to Brian Robison, gritty enough to fight through a shoulder sprain to create the game's only turnover, a third-quarter Aaron Rodgers fumble that Jamarca Sanford emerged from a dogpile clutching.

And Sunday's love belonged to Christian Ponder, who embraced the biggest moments of the biggest game of his life and delivered time after time — 234 yards, three TD passes, no turnovers, a career- best 120.2 rating.

This seemed like a turning point.

Ponder almost threw an interception late in the first half, a Morgan Burnett blitz hit blooping his pass high into the air — like a pop foul behind home plate with at least two Packers waiting to snatch it. Yet somehow Wright turned that into a 17-yard completion.

Later, after Michael Jenkins dropped a potential TD pass with 9:35 left, Ponder came back to him four snaps later for an improvised 3-yard score.

All day, the Vikings turned danger into accomplishment. All season, they've turned belief into success. Now, they're playoff bound. ■

JERRY HOLT, Star Tribune

Sensational Peterson Lifts Team to His Level

A superstar led by example.

By CHIP SCOGGINS/STAR TRIBUNE • December 31, 2012

THE CHANTS reverberated around Adrian Peterson after he ripped off one final breathtaking run.

MVP, MVP, MVP.

The cheers of a delirious and emotionally exhausted grew louder and louder as Peterson's teammates converged on him. Safety Jamarca Sanford threw his arms around Peterson, hoisted him into the air and provided a hero's ride off the field.

What a moment it was, too. Exactly one year to the day after awaking in a hospital bed following major knee surgery, Peterson took a handoff, found his crease and sprinted 26 yards toward history and the playoffs.

"I was definitely trying to get to the end zone by all means," he said.

He didn't quite make it. His storybook run at NFL history fell agonizingly short, but Peterson achieved something even more rewarding and personally satisfying: He willed the Vikings into the playoffs in a season that began without any real expectations for himself or his team.

Peterson's final run Sunday set up Blair Walsh's chip-shot field goal as time expired to give the Vikings a 37-34 victory against the Green Bay Packers, setting up a rematch in the first round of the playoffs Saturday at Lambeau Field.

Needing 208 rushing yards to break Eric Dickerson's single-season rushing record of 2,015, Peterson finished with 199 yards on a career-high 34 carries. That left Peterson's season total at 2,097 -- the second-best mark in league history.

"I know Eric Dickerson is feeling so good right now,"

Peterson said.

Peterson said he didn't keep track of his rushing total during the game or realize how close he came to the record until a few minutes after Walsh's game winner. A touchdown on his final run would have secured it, but the Packers swarmed him at their 11-yard line.

Eight yards short of history.

"It wasn't meant to happen," Peterson said. "Not to say it doesn't hurt because it does, but ultimately we came in here and accomplished the ultimate goal and punched our ticket to the playoffs."

They did so because Peterson provided a season for the ages. He might not have reached Dickerson's mark, but statistics alone don't measure his impact on this team. The Vikings won three games last season and they lost Peterson to a major knee injury. This team was supposed to go nowhere this season, certainly not the postseason.

But Peterson put the Vikings on his broad shoulders and showed them they could achieve more than anyone thought. He gave them hope and confidence. He refused to concede anything, and his teammates followed his lead.

"When you're around greatness," fullback Jerome Felton said, "it raises your level play."

Which is why Peterson should be the league's MVP. Peyton Manning is certainly deserving too, but Peterson breathed life into an entire organization by the way he attacked his rehabilitation and promised to return better than ever. He carried his team to the playoffs in what was supposed to be a rebuilding season. He became only the seventh running back to eclipse 2,000 yards rushing,

even though opponents stacked their defenses to stop him every week.

But nothing stopped him. He was that good. And that motivated. And that special.

He deserves the MVP.

"I don't let awards identify me," he said. "I go out and define myself by what I do on the field. I'm not going to say I don't want to [win], just like I wanted to break the record, but either way, in my heart I'm the MVP. That's all that matters."

Peterson enjoyed his moment in the locker room afterward. Still dressed in uniform, he approached his offensive lineman and personally thanked each one. Former Vikings great Carl Eller stopped by his locker to offer congratulations. Head athletic trainer Eric Sugarman, who oversaw Peterson's rehab, embraced Peterson in a hug. Teammates gushed in all corners of the room.

"Unreal, unbelievable," veteran cornerback Antoine Winfield said. "The greatest running back of all time. Such a special player, special person."

Peterson even joked about having telepathic powers on his 2-yard touchdown catch from Christian Ponder, who apparently let the play develop a little slower than Peterson expected. Or wanted.

"It was like me and Christian were connected," he said. "I was looking at him like, Throw ... The ... Ball! He looked like he was a little unsure if I was going to catch it or not. I was like, throw the ball, run, make a decision now."

Ponder made the right decision. He put the ball in Peterson's hands.

And he delivered, as usual. ▪

CARLOS GONZALEZ, Star Tribune

Vikings' Adrian Peterson Is NFL MVP

Star running back outstripped Peyon Manning for NFL's top award.

By JIM SOUHAN/STAR TRIBUNE • October 12, 2012

NEW ORLEANS — Adrian Peterson brought his whole family to New Orleans to see him win the NFL MVP Award on Saturday night. At least, he brought all he could.

He carried his 18-month-old son, Adrian Jr., who was dressed in a gray three-piece suit. "My little warrior," Peterson called him. He walked with his father and mother. He insisted on remembering a brother.

Brian Peterson died when he was 9, hit by a drunk driver in front of Adrian, who was two years younger. After Peterson became the first Vikings player since Fran Tarkenton in 1975 to win the MVP award, he stood outside the Mahalia Jackson Theater, firmly grasping a trophy and memory. Brian, Adrian said, remains his inspiration whether he's pushing through rehabilitation during a Houston summer, or standing on stage predicting that his first MVP Trophy will not be his last.

"It's always on my mind," Peterson said. "It's constant motivation to just keep fighting. There are times it gets tough. That was a tough situation for me at a young age. I feel like me being able to overcome that made me stronger.

"I feel like dealing with, what, an injury? That's nothing to get through. What compares to losing someone you love, in this life that we live? Not going bankrupt. Not anything. Nothing compares to that. If I'm in a tough situation, I'm always looking at things in that light."

The lights were bright Saturday. Hours after former Vikings receiver Cris Carter was elected to the Hall of Fame, Peterson strolled down the red carpet at the NFL Awards Ceremony, in what would become a televised duel between him and Broncos quarterback Peyton Manning.

After major knee surgery, Peterson rushed for 2,109 yards, nine off the NFL record, while taking the Vikings to the playoffs. After multiple neck surgeries, Manning led the Broncos to the best record in the AFC at 13-3.

Peterson won the Offensive Player of the Year Award. Manning won the Comeback Player of the Year Award. The tiebreaker for major awards would also be most coveted.

Peterson finished with 30 1/2 MVP votes, Manning with 19 1/2. Peterson's ability to dominate defenses massed at the line of scrimmage to stop him made the difference.

"He's a very driven guy, as you know," said Vikings coach Leslie Frazier, who finished third in the Coach of the Year voting, as he stopped on the red carpet before the show. "Adrian felt slighted in not getting the Heisman. He still talks about that. So to be able to get the MVP would be special for him and our organization, and me, personally.

"We all believe he deserves it. He'll be the first to tell you that, too."

A year ago, perhaps only Peterson could have envisioned him recovering from major knee surgery in time to start Game 1, much less in time to become the NFL MVP. A year from now, he plans to win another but refuse to pick it up on time.

"I'm trying to get two or three like Peyton," Peterson said, nodding to Manning, who has won a record four MVP trophies. "Trying to get to your level. But I won't be there to accept it because I'll be winning, with my coach, the most important award, the team award, the Super Bowl."

He looked into the crowd at his large entourage and thanked his father for "putting the ball in my hands." He thanked his mother, a former track star, for his speed. Then he remembered Brian. "Losing my brother ... seeing him get hit by a car right in front of me, that was the toughest," he said.

Peterson left the stage and accepted congratulations from the Who's Who of NFL history gathered in the building. He organized his party and visited a media tent to take a few questions.

Then he stepped outside, exhaled, and admitted that a man known for maniacal preparation didn't write down a single word of his speeches.

"It was an amazing experience," he said. "I'm kind of speechless. I didn't know what to say. I didn't practice a speech. I just thought, if I win, I'll just get through it."

He looked down at the gold trophy, which looked small in his hand. "That's something I can always say: The year I got the MVP, Cris Carter was elected to the Hall of Fame," Peterson said. "What are the odds of that happening?

"That's pretty special. Yeah, that's pretty cool." ■

CARLOS GONZALEZ, Star Tribune

AP's Amazing 2012 Season Rushing Stats

Week	Date	Opp.	Att	Yds	Lg	TD
1	9/9/12	JAC	17	84	20	2
2	9/16/12	IND	16	60	6	0
3	9/23/12	SF	25	86	20	0
4	9/30/12	DET	21	102	18	0
5	10/7/12	TEN	17	88	34	0
6	10/14/12	WAS	17	79	32	0
7	10/21/12	ARI	23	153	27	1
8	10/25/12	TB	15	123	64	1
9	11/4/12	SEA	17	182	74	2
10	11/11/12	DET	27	171	61	1
12	11/25/12	CHI	18	108	23	0
13	12/2/12	GB	21	210	82	1
14	12/9/12	CHI	31	154	51	2
15	12/16/12	STL	24	212	82	1
16	12/23/12	HOU	25	86	21	0
17	12/30/12	GB	34	199	28	1
TOTAL			**348**	**2,097**	-	**12**